Discovering the Law

Discovering the Law

Editor
Sean Butler

Contributors
Sean Butler
Andrew Henderson
Jonathan Herring
Neil Jones
Nicholas McBride
Elaine Palser
Andrej Savin

Published by Law Matters Publishing
Law Matters Limited
33 Southernhay East
Exeter EX1 1NX
Tel: 01392 215577
www.lawmatterspublishing.co.uk

British Library Cataloguing-in-Publication Data

A catalogue record for this book is available from the British Library.

ISBN 10: 1 84641 027 4
ISBN 13: 978 1 84641 027 7

Typeset by Pantek Arts Ltd, Maidstone, Kent

Printed by Ashford Colour Press Ltd, Gosport, Hampshire

Acknowledgements

Sean Butler would like to acknowledge the help and support given to him by his students, RJ Coleman, Hanna Hyry and Darryl Martin, in developing the approach and content of the book.

Contents

7

Contract Law   70
Nicholas J McBride

8

Family Law   79
Jonathan Herring

9

EU Law   88
Dr Andrej Savin

Note on the Contributors

Sean Butler is Fellow and Director of Studies in Law at St Edmund's College, Cambridge, where he teaches Roman Law.

Andrew Henderson is a solicitor in private practice. He was formerly a College Lecturer in Constitutional Law at St Edmund's College, Cambridge.

Jonathan Herring is Fellow in Law at Exeter College, Oxford. He is the author of *Family Law, Criminal Law, Medical Law and Ethics* and *Criminal Law: Text, Cases and Materials*.

Neil Jones is Fellow and Director of Studies in Law at Magdalene College, Cambridge, where he teaches Legal History and Land Law. He is editor of the Journal of Legal History.

Nicholas J McBride is Fellow and Director of Studies in Law at Pembroke College, Cambridge. He is the author of *Letters to a Law Student* (2006) and (with Roderick Bagshaw) *Tort Law* (2nd edn, 2005).

Elaine Palser is a Barrister at 9 Stone Buildings, Lincoln's Inn, London, and a Lecturer in Law at Exeter College, Oxford, where she teaches Trusts and Tort.

Andrej Savin is Fellow in Law at Emmanuel College, Cambridge, where he teaches Private International Law and European Union Law.

Introduction

Dr Sean Butler

Law has always been a popular university degree, both as a stepping stone to working as a lawyer, and to all sorts of work for which legal concepts and techniques are useful. Thus it has value in itself, and for where it can lead.

On the other hand, it is a demanding subject to study, so law students need a high level of commitment. Since law is not widely taught in schools, it is difficult for potential law students to get the flavour of what it is like to study law. There are many good introductory guides which present thorough overviews of legal issues, but which may not fully convey an idea of what a law degree involves, its content, or how law is approached as a university course.

In this book various university lecturers and tutors have presented their observations about the subjects that appear in most law degrees. Each chapter is about a different subject with a brief general introduction and an exploration in depth of specific areas. This gives an understanding of the issues likely to be considered by law students, how the subject is approached, the tools and techiques involved, and shows how interesting the study of law can be.

The nature of legal analysis

Like other courses law teaches techniques of analysis and appraisal, of structure and presentation, but it also teaches a particular style of approach that is based firmly on unreserved engagement with all sides of any issue. It teaches a particular way of looking at things and reporting them. It is discursive in some ways, but in other ways it is brutal in its clarity of analysis, often stripping away the richness of detail and the humanity of the players in order to find the basic structure beneath.

The legal approach teaches caution, and a proper awareness of precedent and previous behaviour, demanding a balanced approach to contradictory viewpoints in which strengths and weaknesses of all sides are exposed. That is not to say that legal writing cannot come down firmly behind a particular stand – doing so is usually a requirement of practising law – but it can produce a rather bloodless conclusion, based on analysis rather than on feeling or passion. Perhaps this is properly so – one does not hire a lawyer for a passionate appraisal but for an impassionate one, a reasoned analysis which considers all aspects.

As a consequence, however, legal methodology can rally all arguments in support of a position, and challenge all arguments against it. As a process to help advance a cause, it can be invaluable. Similarly because of the need to view all sides of an issue, lawyers can be good negotiators and mediators. Their awareness of different positions can help them empathise with different protagonists, and reach solutions that reflect the needs of all parties.

The toolkit for lawyers

The following chapters will show that the law has a broad 'toolkit' of cases and statutes which form the basis of the law, and from which the student learns what the law says. Of course these resources are sometimes ambiguous or obscure, or do not apply completely to the event that has occurred. So there is a need for an exploration of meaning and intent, either at a high conceptual level or at a low pragmatic level, to see what 'the law' actually is. While it may be clear, often it is not, which is why situations end up in court, and why someone, usually a judge, has to make a decision on what the law is in a particular circumstance.

By way of preparation, here is a brief summary.

Cases

For law students and academics, 'cases' usually mean disputes which have resulted in a reported court decision. A case could be a criminal case, where the State brings a charge against a defendant – and the judgment in the case against Mr Smith would be written *R v Smith*, where *R* stands for Regina (the Queen, but in effect, the State) and *v* for versus, or against. Or if it were a civil case, it would usually be between two people or organisations, so a court judgment would be written, for example, *Jones v Brown Engineering Limited*.

Cases are usually reported in journals or reports, such as the All England Law Reports, often written All ER, and of course have a year of publication and volume number, so if the case was at page 120 in volume two in 2006 it would be written as *Jones v Brown Engineering Limited* [2006] 2 All ER 120; other reports include Weekly Law Reports (WLR), Queen's Bench Division (QB), Chancery Division (Ch) and Court of Appeal (AC), and case references are similarly written.

Cases in England and Wales may be heard by one judge, or three or five, and each of them might write a 'judgment', being their analysis of the case and their decision on the outcome. A judgment will often contain a review of the facts, an explanation and analysis of the relevant law, perhaps a review of earlier cases and statutes, an exploration of legal uncertainties, and finally a conclusion. Although a case is usually dealt with by a single judge, if one of the parties appeals against the decision, it will go either to the Court of Appeal or to the House of Lords.

Since the nature of law in England and Wales (and in similar systems – known as 'common law') is that judgments of cases are 'the law', it is normal in legal studies to quote extracts from judgments. So after a quotation by Lord Justice Smith (Smith LJ) on page 130 you might see the reference '(Smith LJ) in *Jones v Brown Engineering Limited* [2006] 2 All ER 120 at 130'.

European Union (EU) cases in the European Court of Justice are reported both with the opinion of the rapporteur (who proposes a judgment to the court) and the judgment itself. The reference will be slightly different from an English case, so would be written, for example, C-120/78 *Cassis de Dijon*.

Statutes

These are in various forms, as the chapters on constitutional law and EU law will show. Statutes are passed by the constitutionally accepted organisation in a country, which in the UK is Parliament. The main types of statutes passed are Acts of Parliament, and regulations. Acts of Parliament are usually more general; regulations more specific and detailed, so in legal studies it is usual to study statutes. A statute is referred to by its name and the year in which it was passed. Part of a statute is termed a section, for example a reference to section 3(1) of the Human Rights Act 1998.

In the EU there are a number of forms of statutes, including Directives and Regulations, again referred to by the name and the year in which they were passed, for example, Council Regulation 2100/94 on Community plant variety rights.

University law courses

Universities offer a wide range of subjects within a law degree, although all law degrees provide a mixture of basic or traditional subjects (such as criminal law and land law) as well as more specialised ones. If a student wishes to qualify as a lawyer in England and Wales (and in some other countries), they need to have studied various basic or 'foundation' subjects: criminal law, tort, contract, land law (property), constitutional law (public law), EU law, and equity, all of which are included in this book.

Whilst studying for a law degree there will also be the opportunity to take other legal subjects as well. For reasons of space, only Roman law and family law are included in this book, but other subjects include international law, commercial law, company law, legal history, conflict of laws, jurisprudence and intellectual property. While jurisprudence is the study of the philosophy of law, and legal history (of course) the history of law, other subjects usually involve similar processes of identifying and exploring laws and cases, seeing how they evolve, how they fit together and how difficult issues can be resolved.

Studying law

Even though the different fields of law may seem intriguing or fascinating or stimulating, studying law at university is not for everyone. It is a demanding subject, with plenty of reading, writing, preparation and presentation, as well as considerable memorising of information. This does not make law unique, of course, but it is an aspect to be considered.

The study of law often involves the usual combinations of lectures and tutorials, and considerable amounts of reading, writing and learning. Written work is often about presenting legal issues, either broadly in an essay or more specifically in an analysis of a 'problem question', designed to contain as many legal nuances and subtleties as possible.

Examinations also usually include essay and problem questions. Essays are, as in other fields, descriptive, and require an ability to remember material and apply it to the question in a structured fashion, with as much detail as can be mustered. Problem questions, on the other hand, require an essentially analytical approach, seeing key parts in the overall complexity, separating them into manageable units, and tackling them with sense, judgment and legal knowledge. In many ways problem questions are the stuff of law. Analysis of the incident, event or transaction upon which advice is required (although rarely in real life with such complexity or coincidences) is enjoyed by some law students, not so much by others.

Whether by essay or problem question the objective is to identify and explore the cases and statutes which make up the law in specific areas. The situation is often clear, but there are also grey areas, for example, where unusual circumstances mean that a word in an Act is ambiguous when considered in that particular context. More commonly, there may be a number of reported cases that lead in slightly different directions. Perhaps none of the cases is quite applicable, so the student has to weigh up the relevance of each case, the different judgments, the circumstances, how recent they are, the seniority of the courts, and the general context. It is in the evaluation of the sources and by reaching some conclusion that the work of the student (and, later on, the practising lawyer) is perhaps at its most iconic and most interesting.

Using a law degree

This book is not intended to be a career guide for law graduates. It is enough to say that a law degree is a good general degree for anyone, which teaches skills of reading and understanding, analysis and judgment, writing and presentation, which will be of value in whatever direction a graduate chooses to go. While qualifying as a lawyer will be attractive to some, for others the law degree will be an excellent foundation for government, industry, NGO or other profession.

The purpose of this book

This book has been written by experienced academics, each writing on a subject which they themselves teach and also conveying why they have found the subject enjoyable, fascinating or stimulating. They are all partisan, of course, but like all good lawyers they also present the challenges and demands of their subject. You may find you enjoy what you read, and want to go further, perhaps to take a law degree – or that you do not, and decide that the study of law is not for you. Either way, the book will have served its purpose.

1 Constitutional Law

Dr Andrew Henderson
St Edmund's College, Cambridge

Introduction

A minister resigns after a sex scandal. The Home Secretary is ordered by a court to release suspected terrorists. A journalist goes to prison for refusing to divulge the source of a story. All of these events involve a rule or principle typically studied in a course on constitutional law.

Often, the first question which the constitutional lawyer has to answer is how it can be said that constitutional law can be a subject as the United Kingdom has no constitution. It is true that there is no single document as in the United States which can be described as 'the constitution'. However, there are numerous materials containing the various rules, principles and practices which, when taken together, can be said to comprise the United Kingdom constitution, or at least to achieve what a constitution is typically designed to achieve. It is the study and analysis of these materials which will occupy the student of constitutional law.

This chapter will give you an idea of why constitutional law is both interesting and important to the study of the law as a whole. We will look at an overview of the United Kingdom constitution and the role of the law in controlling the Government. We will then examine some of the legal questions with which constitutional lawyers have to grapple. We will explore a couple of detailed legal topics – the Royal prerogative as a source of what the Government may or may not do, and a newspaper's intended publication of a story which would disclose government secrets.

The constitution

In unpacking the United Kingdom constitution, we must ask the question: what is a constitution designed to achieve; what is it for? A country's constitution provides the rules and principles which:

(a) provide for the creation and establishment and functioning of the institutions through which the country's citizens may be governed;

(b) govern the relationships of the institutions as between one another; and

(c) govern the relationships of the institutions as between them and the country's citizens.

The institutions themselves will perform three functions:

(a) the legislative function, making the laws under which the people are governed, performed by the legislature or a series of legislatures;

(b) the executive or administrative function, carrying out or administering the law, performed by various executive or administrative agencies;

(c) the judicial function, authoritatively interpreting the law and finally resolving disputes arising under the law, performed by the courts.

Creation and function of institutions

Let us apply the requirements, above, to the United Kingdom, with Parliament, which exercises legislative power (through the Commons, Lords and the Queen), the Government, which exercises executive power (through the Cabinet, civil service, local authorities and regulators), and the courts, which exercise judicial power. Their mere existence indicates that there must be rules for their creation and establishment, but rather than making this assumption, the constitutional lawyer will want to point to a *source* of rules.

Even if there is no *single* written document containing all or the main constitutional rules, the constitutional lawyer may want to show that these rules are written down in various documents created by an assembly of the people, such as in Acts of Parliament. In the United Kingdom there are various Acts of Parliament which can be said to be *constitutional statutes*. *Thoburn v Sunderland City Council* [2002] 3 WLR 247 was a case involving the successful prosecution of traders who refused to use metric measures instead of imperial measures thereby placing them in breach of requirements imposed by European Community law. The Court of Appeal acknowledged that there is a category of statutes known as constitutional statutes. Lord Justice Laws said:

> … a constitutional statute is one which (a) conditions the legal relationship between citizen and State in some general, overarching manner, or (b) enlarges or diminishes the scope of what we would now regard as fundamental constitutional rights.

He included in this category the European Communities Act 1972 which gave effect to the United Kingdom's membership of the European Common Market and by making European law supreme, the Act fundamentally altered the constitutional principle (for the time being, at least) that, in the United Kingdom, Acts of Parliament are supreme.

His definition of a constitutional statute is limited – it does not refer expressly to laws governing the relationship between the institutions of State. More importantly, there is no suggestion that they are specially entrenched: that is, that they require special majorities for their amendment, as opposed to the simple majorities required for the amendment of 'normal statutes', which is the case in those countries which have a supreme constitution. However, it is significant that the idea of constitutional statutes, as a category of statute, was recognised by the *courts* and not by Parliament itself. This emphasises the important role of the courts in determining constitutional rules, particularly in a country with no single constitutional document, either through the interpretation of statutes or development of the common law by applying or adapting earlier judicial decisions to new situations. Even in countries with a single constitutional document, the importance of the courts is recognised by some writers who cynically observe that 'the Constitution is what the judges say it is'. Therefore, the judgments of the courts are a vital source of constitutional rules, and judgments form a very large part of constitutional law.

The sources of constitutional rules

As regards legislative institutions, the Acts and Treaty of Union between Scotland and England of 1707 and associated legislation can be said to contain the origins of the modern Parliament at Westminster. Its functioning is governed mainly by the Parliament Acts of 1911 and 1949 which, for example, determine the maximum length of time between general elections and the procedures for enacting primary legislation. These Acts are not confined to the more prosaic world of parliamentary practice. In seeking to challenge the validity of the fox hunting ban brought into law by the Hunting Act 2004, the Countryside Alliance unsuccessfully challenged the validity of the 1949 Parliament Act under which the 2004 Act had been passed. (See *R (on the application of Jackson) v Attorney-General* [2005] 3 WLR 733.) Legislation also governs the composition of the Parliament at Westminster, including the more recent House of Lords Act 1999, which abolished the rights of hereditary peers to sit in the House of Lords. The programme of constitutional reform also included devolution for Scotland and Wales. The Scotland Act 1998 and Government of Wales Act 1998 created the Scottish Parliament and Welsh Assembly, respectively.

For the judicial institutions the Supreme Court 1981 governs the powers of the High Court, which includes the powers of judicial review, and the Constitutional Reform Act 2005 includes provisions dealing with the creation of a Supreme Court (the United Kingdom's highest court) and the appointment of judges.

Locating the sources of rules governing the operation of the executive is less straightforward. The monarch, as head of State, is governed by various statutes, for example the Regency Act 1937 which deals with the carrying out of the monarch's functions in the event of his or her incapacity. However, the other important executive institutions such as the Prime Minister, the Cabinet and the civil service have not come into being as result of statute. Instead they have arisen through *constitutional convention*, that is, they have arisen through constitutional usage or practice.

A constitutional convention is a binding rule of constitutional behaviour. Although conventions have been acknowledged by the courts, they are not enforced by the courts. Instead, conventions derive their force from the political consequences which flow from their breach, eg possible loss office, and by the fact that, generally, those who are subject to a convention will simply feel, for reasons of constitutional tradition or propriety, that they ought not to depart from the convention.

The fact that constitutional conventions are studied as part of constitutional law, as an important set of constitutional rules, highlights a key aspect of constitutional law which probably sets it apart from most other fields of law: politics. An in-depth understanding of British politics is not necessary for a proper understanding of the functioning of the United Kingdom constitution. Nor, and perhaps more importantly, is an in-depth understanding of British politics an effective substitute for an understanding of the operation of the rules of the United Kingdom constitution. However, a basic understanding of the context in which these rules operate is necessary in order to examine more critically the distinction between the 'political constitution' and the 'legal constitution' and the extent to which the United Kingdom constitution is shifting from the former to the latter.

Relationships of institutions between one another

The second purpose of a constitution is to govern the relationships of the institutions as between one another. A vital aspect of these relationships, and one that is central to a study of constitutional law, is the check on or control of one institution by another. This is also a key aspect of the doctrine of the separation of powers, and the main issue often studied in relation to the doctrine of the separation of powers is the extent to which the United Kingdom constitution can be said to adhere to the doctrine.

We have described Parliament as a legislative institution. However, there is more to Parliament than its law-making function. Parliament supplies the Government with its ministers as well as supplying it with money to carry out its functions. Having supplied the Government with its ministers, Parliament is responsible for keeping a check on the ministers. This is achieved, or sought to be achieved, via the constitutional convention of collective and ministerial accountability. This means that ministers must account and be responsible to both chambers of Parliament – Commons and Lords – of the House and to the various parliamentary select committees, for their development and implementation of government policy, government administration and government expenditure.

In addition to the political mechanism for checking the power of the executive, the courts' powers of judicial review provide the primary legal mechanism for keeping a check on the executive. Judicial review is potentially vast as a topic for study and may be studied in more detail during a course on administrative law together with the study of other control mechanisms such as ombudsmen, and other legal remedies, such as claims for damages against administrative bodies.

The basis for judicial review can be found in s 31 of the Supreme Court Act 1981 and the Civil Procedure Rules 1998. However the substance of the law and, more particularly, the standards against which the legality of government administration is measured have mainly been developed by the courts, although Parliament has made some important contributions, particularly in relation to human rights, as we shall see below. When a court reviews the administration of governmental power it will examine whether the administrator has acted within its powers, the bounds of which are determined by the law. Generally, the court will need to determine these bounds by first examining the relevant statute under which the powers are exercised and determining whether the administrator is acting within the 'four corners' of that statute.

The analysis does not end there. The court will also ask whether the administrator has acted in accordance with various principles developed by the court in the course of inter-preting the scope of the powers conferred by statutes. Therefore, for example, in addition to asking whether the decision of an administrator, Adam, to refuse to continue to fund Bob's university education under the (fictional) University Funding Act 2006 falls outside the express language of the Act, the court will also ask whether Bob has been given the opportunity to put his case to Adam as to why the funding should continue. Even if the University Funding Act does not expressly state that Bob has the right to be heard, in the absence of language which states that Bob does *not* have the right to be heard, the courts will presume that Parliament intended there to be such a right. If the court finds Adam ought to have given Bob the opportunity to put his case before Adam took the decision, the court has the power to set aside the decision by making a 'quashing order' and return-ing the matter to Adam to take the decision again, with an order that Adam hear what Bob has to say before making the decision. (A court in judicial review proceedings may make other orders, such as prohibitory orders (prohibiting an act) or mandatory orders (requiring an act).)

The orders which the court may make in such a case tell us something about the nature and limits of judicial review. Judicial review does not permit a court to make a decision regarding the *merits* of an administrative decision but only the *legality* of the decision: the court is not concerned with *what* was decided but *how* the decision was reached. To follow the example above, if Adam allows Bob to put his case to Adam but reaches the same decision as above, provided that the decision is reasonable and proportionate (which we will examine below) and is within the express provisions of the University Funding Act, a court would not have the power to set aside the decision, even if the court disagreed with Adam's decision.

Relationships between institutions and citizens

The example above also highlights the role of judicial review as a mechanism for giving effect to the third purpose of a constitution: to govern the relationships of the institutions as between them and the country's citizens. The primary constitutional device for ensuring that the State respects the rights and freedoms of its citizens is a bill of rights which is capable of being enforced by the courts.

The United Kingdom does not have a single, domestic document similar to, for example, the amendments to the United States Constitution which comprise its Bill of Rights. (The Bill of Rights 1689 was concerned with the constitutional arrangements between the Crown and Parliament rather than with the rights and freedoms of individuals.) Instead, the United Kingdom law of civil liberties and human rights has developed through a com-bination of statutory and judge-made rules. The closest which the United Kingdom comes to having a bill of rights is the Human Rights Act 1998, included in the catalogue of con-stitutional statutes by Lord Justice Laws in *Thoburn v Sunderland City Council* (2002). The Human Rights Act 1998 seeks to protect individual rights and freedoms by incorporating the main provisions of the European Convention on Human Rights into United Kingdom law. These include the protection of the rights to life, security of the person, access to the courts and privacy, the protection of the freedoms of expression, religion and assembly, and the prohibition against torture.

The 1998 Act governs the relationship between the individual and the executive institutions of State, giving force to these protections in the United Kingdom, through s 6(1) which states: 'It is unlawful for a public authority to act in a way which is not compatible with a Convention right'. Under s 8 a court which finds that a public authority has acted unlawfully 'may grant such relief or remedy … which it considers just and appropriate'. In addition to the power to quash a decision mentioned above, this would include the power to award damages. The Act also gives the courts the power to declare that an Act of Parliament is incompatible with convention rights, although the courts do not have the power to invalidate an Act in these circumstances, thereby leaving intact the doctrine of parliamentary sovereignty.

Some examples of constitutional law in practice

The royal prerogative

As we have already seen, a central concern of constitutional law is the control of the powers of the executive. In order to control power, it is necessary to identify the source of that power. In the United Kingdom there are two sources of executive power: statute and the royal prerogative. The fact that the powers exercised under the royal prerogative have not been placed on a statutory footing is itself a source of debate amongst constitutional scholars. As one way of examining the royal prerogative, we will consider the following question: should those powers capable of being exercised under the royal prerogative be placed on a statutory basis and limited to those powers identified in that statute?

We start with the definition of the royal prerogative. In his *Commentaries on the Laws of England* (1765), the eighteenth-century jurist, Blackstone, described the prerogative as: ' … in its nature singular and eccentrical [in] that it can only be applied to those discretionary or arbitrary rights and capacities which the king enjoys alone … and not to those which he enjoys in common with any of his subjects'. For Blackstone the prerogative is a closed list of identifiable powers which can only be exercised by the Crown. (In practice the powers are exercised by the executive, ie ministers, in the name of the Crown.) Importantly, the prerogative may not simply be relied on when the Government cannot find a statutory power to justify its action. This definition can be contrasted with that of the Victorian jurist, Dicey, in *Introduction to the Study of the Law of the Constitution* (1885), who described the prerogative as the 'residue of discretionary or arbitrary authority which at any time is legally left in the hands of the Crown'.

Dicey's more expansive view of the prerogative was accepted in *R v Criminal Injuries Board, ex p Lain* [1967] 2 QB 864 where the Court of Appeal recognised that the Government had the power to establish the Criminal Injuries Compensation Board without statutory authority to make *ex gratia* payments to the victims of crime, despite the fact that such a power fell within Parliament's jurisdiction (the Board was reconstituted under the Criminal Justice Act 1988) and that the power was not unique to the Crown because individuals can also give away money. Moreover, in *R v Secretary of State for the Home Department, ex p Northumbria Police Authority* [1989] QB 26, the Court of Appeal recognised that the Secretary of State's power to issue police with plastic bullets and CS gas without approval of the local police authority could be justified both under statute and under the prerogative. However, the nature of the particular prerogative in question was far from clear. There are precedents for the exercise of prerogative power to protect the realm from external attack. However, authority for the exercise of prerogative power to keep the peace within the realm is less clear. Even if such a prerogative does exist, before the *Northumbria Police Authority* case there was no authority for extending this power to arm the police with plastic bullets and CS gas.

The *Northumbria Police Authority* case indicates that, in principle, where it deems it expedient, the executive can assume a power for itself, even where (a) there is no clear precedent for the exercise of such power and (b) Parliament has not granted it that power. This is bad for the Constitution which is concerned with the control of power. If the source or nature of a power, such as the royal prerogative, is not clearly identifiable or subject to the stricter definition offered by Blackstone, it becomes easier for the executive to justify the exercise of that power and more difficult for the courts to control it. One solution, therefore, is for Parliament to identify the prerogative powers which the executive can exercise.

This would be achieved by identifying and limiting, that is, codifying those powers in an Act of Parliament. The executive would, therefore, have to identify the particular power which it sought to exercise in the relevant Act. If the power was not identified in the Act, the executive would have to ask Parliament to amend or extend the Act to grant it the power, rather than assuming that power itself.

As to the prerogative powers which would need to be codified, the list is wide and diverse with the following being the most important powers: those relating to foreign affairs, namely the power to make declarations of war and peace, the power to enter into treaties, the recognition of foreign states, diplomatic relations and disposition of the armed forces overseas; and those relating to domestic affairs, namely the summoning and dissolution of Parliament, the appointment of ministers, the royal assent to Bills, the granting of honours, the defence of the realm, the keeping of the peace, the *parens patriae* jurisdiction of the courts, the power to stop criminal prosecutions, the reduction of sentences, the pardoning of offenders, the regulation of the terms and conditions of the civil service and the right to royal fish and swans.

The broad and diverse nature of the powers exercised under the prerogative suggests that a single Act might not be sufficient, but rather a number of Acts would be appropriate. In addition to identifying and limiting prerogative powers, an Act of Parliament could also make provision for the control by Parliament of the exercise of prerogative powers. For example, the Act could require the consent of Parliament for the executive to declare war, similar to the War Powers Act in the United States.

The arguments for codifying the royal prerogative can be contrasted with those against doing so. First, providing the executive with a broad source of residual powers allows for flexibility and efficiency, thus according with one of the central characteristics of the United Kingdom constitution. Secondly, even if the prerogative powers were set out in a statute, the words defining and describing those powers would still need to be interpreted by the executive and by the courts. The executive could argue that the exercise of a particular power ('power A') was either implied by the words describing a prerogative power ('power B') or that the exercise of power A was necessary for the exercise of power B despite the fact that power A was not set out in the Act. Thirdly, the exercise of prerogative powers is subject to political power in so far as an unpopular exercise of prerogative power, such as a decision to go to war, could lead to a reduction in support for the Government (the decision to go to war in Iraq in 2003 is a good example).

In addition, the exercise of prerogative power is subject to control by the courts: in principle, the courts have the same powers of judicial review over powers exercised under the prerogative as they do over powers exercised pursuant to statute. (In practice, however, the courts may not be as willing to exercise their powers of review over many of the prerogatives. In *Council of Civil Service Unions v Minister for the Civil Service* [1985] AC 374, the Judicial Committee of the House of Lords indicated that matters such as the appointment of ministers, dissolution of Parliament, the grant of honours, treaties and matters of national security were not appropriate subjects for judicial review.) With regard to control by the courts, with the advent of the Human Rights Act 1998 the exercise of any power of a member of the executive, in so far as that member of the executive is a person certain whose functions are functions of a public nature (see s 6(3)(b) of the Act), must be in a way which is not incompatible with a Convention right (see s 6(1)). This means that, despite the fact that the source of a prerogative power is not statutory, there is an all-encompassing *statute* in the form of the Human Rights Act, which imposes the same standards on the exercise of executive powers under the prerogative as it does on the exercise of executive powers under statute.

The arguments for and against codification of the royal prerogative are evenly balanced and the outcome of the debate hinges on the extent to which one seeks to insist on strict, properly defined legal standards or whether one is willing to tolerate more flexibility in the knowledge that there are some political and legal controls on the abuse of powers exercised under the prerogative. This, in turn, highlights the fundamental constitutional issues already discussed. It indicates how a discrete constitutional topic can touch broad issues studied throughout the course.

Official secrecy

We now turn to official secrecy, a topic which falls within the third purpose of constitutional law: the relationship between the individual and the State. This topic is relevant to this relationship in that it deals with the extent to which the State can prevent the individual from disclosing confidential information. It is, in turn, related to the individual's freedom of expression where the individual wishes to make the information available to a wide audience, for example, by publishing the information in a newspaper. In this case, we will use a practical problem.

Assume that the Government has dispatched troops to Equatoria, allegedly as part of an international effort to crush terrorism and restore order to the country after an attempted *coup d'état* and in order to protect British citizens in Equatoria. Adam, a senior civil servant at the Ministry of Defence, believes that British troops have been sent to Equatoria by irresponsible and deceitful ministers in order to protect the construction of a nuclear power plant in a neighbouring territory by the company, Britpower. Wishing to expose the ministers, he sends a confidential memorandum to Bob, editor of the *Daily Gossip*, revealing certain aspects of the military planning. The *Daily Gossip* publishes an editorial condemning the Government's intervention in Equatoria, claiming that the real reason for the intervention is the protection of the interests of Britpower, which the *Daily Gossip* alleges has made large donations to the political party which is currently in power. You are asked to advise the Attorney-General on whether: (i) Adam can be successfully prosecuted for breaches of the criminal law and (ii) Bob can be successfully prosecuted for breaches of the criminal law.

In his essay, 'Confidentiality', in *Freedom of Expression and Freedom of Information* (Oxford: Oxford University Press, 2000), Lord Scott, a judge of the House of Lords, identifies the following principle as one which underlies the law of confidentiality: the Government is not entitled to protection from disclosure of confidential information about itself unless there is a sufficient public interest requiring the protection from disclosure of information. In essence, the Government is limited to restricting the freedom of an individual to publicise information about the Government. In the case of official secrets, it can be argued that it is in the public interest for the Government to be able to function in an efficient manner by controlling the flow of information in order to prevent access to certain official decisions, particularly those relating to national security, and in order to be able to release information selectively and at convenient moments. The Official Secrets Act 1989 facilitates this by criminalising the disclosure of certain types of information.

Turning first to the position of Adam, s 2(1) of the 1989 Act states:

> A person who is or has been a Crown servant or government contractor is guilty of an offence if without lawful authority he makes a damaging disclosure of any information, document or other article relating to defence which is or has been in his possession by virtue of his position as such.

Section 2(2) indicates that a disclosure will be damaging if:

> (a) it damages the capability of, or any part of, the armed forces of the Crown to carry out their tasks or leads to loss of life or injury to members of those forces or serious damage to the equipment or installations of those forces; or (b) otherwise than as mentioned in paragraph (a) above, it endangers the interests of the United Kingdom abroad, seriously obstructs the promotion or protection by the United Kingdom of those interests or endangers the safety of British citizens abroad; or (c) it is of information or of a document or article which is such that its unauthorised disclosure would be likely to have any of those effects.

Section 2(1) applies to Adam: he is a Crown servant which, in terms of s 12 of the Act, includes 'any person employed in the civil service of the Crown' (see s 12(1)(c)). Moreover, the information dealing with aspects of the military planning should fall within the meaning of section 2: according to the official explanation, the intervention in Equatoria is intended to protect British citizens there. It cannot be said, on the facts presented, that Adam's disclosure to Bob will, as a matter of fact, cause the type of damage required by s 2(2)(a) or 2(2)(b). However, the nature of the information disclosed is such that, at a minimum, its disclosure would be likely to obstruct seriously the promotion or protection of the United Kingdom in Equatoria, thus bringing it within s 2(2)(c): Adam disclosed the information to a journalist who, by definition, has the ability to disseminate the information widely.

Adam's disclosure to Bob would be likely to damage the work of, or any part of the security or intelligence services. Finally, Adam does not appear to have disclosed the information to Bob in accordance with his official duty as a senior civil servant at the Ministry of Defence (indicating that the disclosure does not fall within s 7 of the Act, which deals with authorised disclosures). His activities should, therefore, fall within s 2 of the 1989 Act.

The existence of any defence to the offence in s 2(1) needs to be considered. Section 2(3) of the Act states:

> It is a defence for a person charged with an offence under this section to prove that at the time of the alleged offence he did not know, and had no reasonable cause to believe, that the information, document or article in question related to defence or that its disclosure would be damaging within the meaning of subsection (1) above.

On the facts presented, it is difficult to see how Adam could show that he did not know that the information related to defence – he is a senior member of the Ministry of Defence. As regards whether Adam knew, or ought reasonably to have known, that disclosure of the information would be damaging, on the facts presented it is more difficult to determine whether this is the case. However, the fact that the information was confidential would tend to suggest that its disclosure would be damaging; if not, why keep it confidential? In any event, this fact ought not to prevent the bringing of a prosecution against Adam under the 1989 Act, although the success of such a prosecution can only be more fully advised on once more facts are provided.

Official secrecy is also affected by the Human Rights Act 1998: s 3(1) of the Human Rights Act 1998 requires the Official Secrets Act 1989, as far as it is possible to do so, to be read and given effect to in a way which is compatible with Convention rights, including freedom of expression enshrined in Article 10 of the European Convention on Human Rights. Could Adam argue that he believed that, by disclosing the information to Bob, he was exercising his freedom of expression and, in so doing, acting in the public interest by exposing the Government to public scrutiny? In such circumstances and giving s 2 of the Official Secrets Act a meaning that is compatible with Art 10 of the Convention, could Adam not argue that his behaviour simply does not fall within s 2 and that he should be acquitted? Alternatively, that s 2 was incompatible with Art 10?

An argument similar to this was considered by the House of Lords in *R v Shayler* [2003] 1 AC 247 which involved the publication of an article written by David Shayler, a former member of the security service, which, according to the prosecution, related to matters of security and intelligence, the unauthorised disclosure of which is governed by ss 1 and 4 of the Official Secrets Act 1989. The House of Lords rejected the argument that ss 1 and 4 were in breach of Art 10 on the basis that Mr Shayler had other avenues to make the disclosures in question, ie by requesting permission from his employers to make the disclosure. The refusal by his employers to permit the disclosure would have been subject to judicial review. It is likely that the same reasoning would apply in the context of s 2, discussed earlier. Therefore, the Attorney-General could proceed with a prosecution of Adam.

Turning to Bob, s 5 of the Official Secrets Act 1989 deals with information resulting from unauthorised disclosures. Section 5(2) states:

the person into whose possession the information, document or article [protected against disclosure by section 2 of the Act and disclosed to him by a Crown servant or government contractor without lawful authority] has come is guilty of an offence if he discloses it without lawful authority knowing, or having reasonable cause to believe, that it is protected against disclosure [by section 2 of the Act and has been disclosed to him by a Crown servant or government contractor without lawful authority].

In order for a person to commit the offence in s 5(2), s 5(3) requires that

(a) the disclosure by him is damaging; and

(b) he makes it knowing, or having reasonable cause to believe, that it would be damaging ... .

Section 5(2) applies to Bob: he has received the information from Adam, who has acted in breach of s 2. Section 5(2) will require the prosecution to show that Bob knew that the information was protected by s 2 of the Act. On the facts here, the prosecution should be able to show this – the information is of a sensitive nature and has not been disclosed. However, it is not clear how much information has actually been disclosed in the editorial, nor the extent to which the editorial has damaged or is likely to damage British interests in Equatoria. Therefore, further investigation would be necessary before a prosecution could be recommended.

Reading list

E Barendt, *An Introduction to Constitutional Law* (Oxford: Oxford University Press, 1998).
A Tomkins, *Public Law* (Oxford: Oxford University Press, 2003).
T Wright, *British Politics: A Very Short Introduction* (Oxford: Oxford University Press, 2003).

2 Roman Law

Dr Sean Butler
St Edmund's College, Cambridge
(with a revised translation from the Digest by
Professor John Crook, St John's College, Cambridge)

Introduction

Some 2,000 years ago Roman legislators, jurists and magistrates developed a wide range of concepts, rights, remedies and structures that can still be seen in current legal systems. Roman law itself has been the foundation of civil law applied through much of Europe and outside (though not of the common law of England), as well as establishing many of the rules and principles of law which today we take for granted. To study Roman law is to observe modern legal concepts as they were being created, explored and developed.

Rome was essentially a lightly regulated, free-market economy which allowed its citizens substantial freedom in the conduct of their affairs. As a result, laws were developed which reflected that freedom and enabled it to be enforced in the courts. The Roman citizen, therefore, enjoyed laws on marriage and death, owning and selling land and goods, hiring and employment, that are easily recognisable today. Although the period commonly studied is far in the past – the Classical period of Roman law lasted from say 27 BC to AD 224 – and the conduct of Roman citizens of the time would often seem unusual to the point of being brutal, one can still enjoy considerable resonance with Romans and their laws.

The purpose of this chapter is to discuss some elements of a typical university Roman law course, and to give some idea of why it is exciting. There is a brief history of Rome during the Classical period, and in particular the development of Roman law. Three topics will be explored in detail: how to enforce a contract with a slave; when you would be liable for injuring someone; and how to protect the view from your window.

Historical background

The perceived heritage of the Romans was that Rome was founded in the eighth century BC by Romulus and Remus, descendants of Aeneas, a hero of Troy. Ruled initially by kings, the Republic was established in about 510 BC and many of its elements – particularly the Senate and the Consuls – were also significant in the Roman constitution.

By the start of the Classical period, the Roman Empire had been in some political disorder for a century. Checks and balances, supposedly secured by dividing power among the two Consuls, the Senate and the assemblies, were falling aside and instead the Republic was dominated by men from rich and powerful aristocratic families with the support of the army. The first triumvirate, of Julius Caesar, Pompey and Crassus, started the shift towards a more powerful autocratic government, culminating in the success of Augustus (formerly known as Octavian), adopted son of Julius Caesar, and marking the beginning of the period known as the 'Empire'. Augustus can be seen as providing a more stable alternative – although no more democratic – to what had preceded, and in fact his period of some 40 years as Emperor was largely safe and prosperous (except for those who opposed him, and as a result were executed or dispossessed).

The Empire went through inevitable vicissitudes during the next few hundred years, with Emperors such as Nero and Claudius, Marcus Aurelius and Commodus, helping and harming the Empire according to their skills and weaknesses. In the third century AD the Emperor Diocletian separated the Empire into the East and the West, and when his successor, Constantine, became Emperor he established in AD 330 a new capital at Byzantium, modestly renamed Constantinople (and now known as Istanbul). In the following two centuries the Western Empire gradually disintegrated and became overrun, while the Eastern Empire remained broadly powerful and survived into the eighth century and beyond.

For much of the Classical period Rome was prosperous, stable and economically vigorous. It controlled diverse regions and most of the countries around the Mediterranean, and so had a rich mixture of peoples and goods, living and working under the *pax Romana* – the peace provided from and by Rome. The richness and diversity were reflected in the city itself; much of it was architecturally grand and spacious, and there were well over a million people living there. Just like today's modern city there were houses and blocks of flats, shops, bars and restaurants – as well as chariot teams to support, gladiatorial displays, circuses, and plays to watch. There were bathhouses for leisure and exercise, nightclubs and fashionable parties. It was a vibrant city, with much that is recognised today, separated more by technology than by character; you would understand the Romans.

Legal background

A study of Roman law is partly constrained by available materials – a lot of legal writing is no longer around, and much of the rest is affected to some degree by uncertainty about its reliability. The first key legal document, largely lost, is known as the Twelve Tables, written in about 450 BC. The Twelve Tables, probably setting out many of the customary laws of the city and some legal procedure, appears to have been the first time that legal rights and remedies were set out plainly for all citizens to read and use. Before then, legal procedures were known only to the priests.

Law in subsequent years came from a number of legislative and executive and private sources, forming an evolutionary story. During the Republic there was a certain amount of legislation in a formal sense, passed by one of the assemblies, but much more important was the effective contribution to the law by the praetors, magistrates who were responsible for managing the court process. When the process of litigation developed a more flexible system in the late second century BC (the *formulary system*), the impact of the praetors on law-making increased significantly.

The praetors were in office for only one year, and at the start of their term they published their remedies, or edicts, which set out the types of claims they would accept. This was law-making (and known as the *ius honorarium*), because they decided when a remedy would be granted and *ubi remedium, ibi ius* – where there is a remedy, there is a right. Thus by their remedies they could extend or limit the existing law, for example by recognising a right that the existing law did not recognise, or by extending a right beyond the limits of the legislation (as in *Lex Aquilia*, discussed below). The result of praetorian law-making was that a series of distinct remedies or *actiones* evolved, usually dealing with specific types of activities, such as *actio empti* for a sale or *actio locati* for a hire.

The creative authority of the praetors became more limited by the second century AD (and was largely halted in about AD 135 when the edict was codified by Julian for the Emperor Hadrian), but by then a further source of law had emerged: the jurists – private individuals who commented and advised on the law, and who taught and wrote about it. Despite the significant law-making power of the praetors they were generally not lawyers, and often relied on jurists (legal advisors) to guide them. Although we only know about the works of a handful of jurists, by their work and their writing they were able to provide a structure for the law, defining concepts and principles by which law could be described and discussed; now it could develop, becoming more sophisticated and embracing new concepts as it did so. The work of the jurists, and particularly debate between them, arguably made the most important contribution to Roman law.

The concepts and principles of the jurists might, however, have been lost without the achievement of the Emperor Justinian in the mid-sixth century, who produced a compendium of the law known as the 'Digest'. This contained extracts from the most important jurists such as Paul, Ulpian, Gaius and Modestinus, who lived during the first to third centuries AD (and the extracts in this chapter are sections from the Digest, hence the letter 'D.'). Apart from the Digest, the only work to survive in full is a student textbook called the 'Institutes' written in about AD 160 by the jurist Gaius.

In their works, jurists often explored situations – either real, or case studies – and then set out the legal consequences. As is commonly the case with legal writing, books were written which explained and discussed the law on a particular topic or field. The jurists' work could be based on existing law, such as in this extract from Paul:

> It is provided by the Rhodian Law [of the sea] that where merchandise is thrown overboard for the purpose of lightening a ship, what has been lost for the benefit of all must be made up by the contribution of all. *Paul, D.14.2.1*

Often, however, jurists would simply state the law:

> If a man has not killed a slave or an animal but has burnt, broken, or injured, proceedings can undoubtedly be taken under this provision of the law. Therefore, if you throw a torch at my slave and burn him, you will be liable to me. *Ulpian, D.9.2.27.6*

At the same time as the jurists were making their fundamental contribution to the development of law, more formal legislation was starting to have a greater impact. The power of the Emperor to legislate was growing strongly through his edicts, as well as through judicial decisions and legal answers (*decreta* and *rescripta*), and *senatusconsulta* of the

and Chapter 3 dealt with other forms of injury to cattle, slaves and to anything (and anybody) else:

> If anyone damages the property of another in cases other than killing slaves or cattle, by burning, breaking or tearing off unlawfully, whatever the property was worth in the nearest thirty days, so much he must be ordered to pay to the owner. *Ulpian, D.9.2.27.5*

Despite their simplicity, from a legal point of view these two chapters raise a number of interesting issues of uncertainty of meaning – which are inevitable when applying law to a specific situation. The uncertainty can be resolved (or at least limited) by a number of approaches, including understanding the meaning of the words used, the purpose of the laws, the intention behind them, the need for similar situations to be treated in the same way – and correspondingly for different situations to be distinguished.

For example, Gaius interpreted the words 'a quadruped included in the class of cattle' in Chapter 1 by exploring the characteristics which distinguished cattle from other animals:

> ... animals which are included under the head of cattle, and are kept in herds, as, for instance, sheep, goats, oxen, horses, mules, and asses. The question arises whether hogs are included under the designation of cattle, and it is very properly decided by Labeo that they are. Dogs, however, do not come under this head; much less are wild beasts included, as for instance, bears, lions, and panthers. Elephants and camels are, as it were, mixed, for they perform the labour of beasts of burden, and yet their nature is wild, therefore they must be included ... *Gaius, D.9.2.2.2*

Ulpian explored the nature of damage in an action under Chapter 3:

> ... it is evident that suit can be brought under the *Lex Aquilia* where a party puts filth in wine, or spills it, or turns it into vinegar or spoils it in any other way; for both pouring it out and turning it into vinegar are included in the words 'destroy' ... We must, by all means, understand that the expression is applicable where a party wounds a slave, or strikes him with a stick, or a strap, or with his fist, or with a weapon, or with anything else which would cut or raise a swelling upon the body of anyone ... *Ulpian, D.9.2.27.15, 17*

While these are essentially straightforward interpretations, not especially different from modern statutory interpretation, other situations raise more complex issues: such as where something has been damaged, but the goods themselves were unharmed, for example, some sand is mixed with grain and they cannot be separated – the load of grain is clearly damaged, but the grain itself is unharmed. Ulpian treated it in the same way as destruction:

> Again, where anyone mixes sand or something else with wheat, so that it is difficult to separate it, proceedings can be brought against him just as if he had spoiled it. *Ulpian, D.9.2.27.20*

The situation is clearly analogous to damage, and arguing that the individual grains have not been damaged would be foolish. One problem in any interpretation of a law is to decide how far the meaning of its words can be understood: this involves consideration about the purpose and extent of the law, how far it should go to ensure fair treatment of factually different but legally similar situations – and that consideration does not necessarily produce a consensus. In interpreting the *Lex Aquilia*, sometimes the jurists felt the law would not apply even though the circumstances demanded similar treatment, and a separate but comparable remedy was introduced by the praetors (probably on the advice of jurists) known as an *actio in factum* (or an *actio utilis*). The *actio in factum* would be used where, for example, there was indirect harm or loss without damage.

Indirect harm was where the assailant effectively caused the harm, though he actually did something else which in turn caused the harm. Although the distinction between two situations below proposed by Ulpian seems trivial – the difference between administering a fatal drug and giving it to the victim to take themselves – it was legally important (and is still currently relevant in considering the contrast between causing death by withholding treatment from terminally ill patients, and the administration of fatal treatment):

> Moreover, where a midwife administers a drug to a woman and she dies in consequence, Labeo makes a distinction, namely: that if she administered it with her own hands she should be held to have killed, but if she gave it to the woman in order that she might take it herself, an *actio in factum* should be granted, and this opinion is correct; for she rather provided the cause of death, than actually killed. *Ulpian, D.9.2.9*

Similarly where something has been lost but not actually damaged, Ulpian supported the view that an *actio in factum* would be granted:

> If anyone has knocked coins out of my hand, Sabinus is of the opinion that an action for wrongful injury will lie, if they are lost in such a way that they cannot come into anyone's possession, as for instance, where they have fallen into a river, the sea, or a sewer. *Ulpian, D.9.2.27.21*

Finally, there are the interesting situations where someone consents to do harm to him- or herself, and so cannot properly complain about it. A boxer in the ring is an obvious case which was considered by the jurists, although they treated it under the concept of fault or *culpa* and so the issue in Roman law was whether there was *culpa* by the assailant, rather than consent by the victim:

> Where in a wrestling match or in a wrestling plus boxing contest or where two boxers are engaged, someone kills another; if it was in a public contest, the *Lex Aquilia* will not apply, because the damage must be considered to have been committed for the sake of renown and courage, and not with the intent to cause injury. *Ulpian, D.9.2.7.4*

Again the jurists were presenting a single factual situation, but enabling us – and Roman lawyers – to understand the nature and the breadth of the law. The principle could be extended, so that if you went to a dangerous place you did so at your own risk:

> ... but where persons are practising with javelins, and a slave crosses the place the *Lex Aquilia* will not apply, because he should not have rashly crossed the field where this practice was going on. *Ulpian, D.9.2.9.4*

In effect, if you practised throwing javelins in the proper place to do so, and someone crossed the field and was injured, then you were not at fault and so not liable, you did not have the necessary *culpa* (unless of course you intended to impale the person). This illustrates a point about how the law develops, which is working by analogy: considering previous cases and deciding whether the same decision would be reached with slightly different facts, and how different the facts must be for the decision to change. In the case described above, the dangerous activity is carried out in a proper place, but what if the place were not appropriate, perhaps by a highway or public path, or if the activity was not as dangerous as javelin-throwing? It was discussed by Paul:

> Where a trimmer of trees throwing down a branch, or a man working on an elevation, kills a passer-by, he is only liable if it fell in a public place, and he did not give warning, that the accident might be avoided. Mucius, however, states that even if this happened on private property, an action could be brought for negligence; because it is negligence when provision was not made by taking such precautions as a diligent man would have done, or warning was only given when the danger could not have been avoided. On this principle it does not make much difference whether the party injured was crossing public or private ground, since it very frequently happens that many persons go through private ground. If there is no roadway there, the party is only liable for malice in that he must not throw something down on anyone whom he can see is passing by; for he cannot be held accountable for negligence, as he would be unable to foresee whether anyone is going to pass through that place or not. *Paul, D.9.2.31*

To close, a more unusual example of responsibility or *culpa*, where someone has a shave beside a ball game:

> ... Mela writes that if, while several persons are playing ball, the ball having been struck too violently should fall upon the hand of a barber who is shaving a slave at the time, in such a way that the throat of the latter is cut by the razor; the party responsible for negligence is liable under the *Lex Aquilia*. Proculus thinks that the barber is to blame; and, indeed, if he had the habit of shaving persons in a place where it is customary to play ball, or where there was much travel, some blame can be attached to him; although it may not improperly be held that where anyone seats himself in a barber's chair in a dangerous place, he has only himself to blame. *Ulpian, D.9.2.11*

Urban praedial servitudes (protecting the view from your window)

Having a nice view out of the window, and wanting to avoid a building or wall blocking that view, are concerns both modern and Roman, and similarly the concept of servitudes developed by Roman law (now the law of easements) is still applicable. Servitudes are types of benefit and burden, and in Roman law there were two main types: 'personal' and 'praedial'. 'Personal servitudes' affected people, for example, the right to occupy a house for life, while 'praedial servitudes' affected land (from the Latin, *praedium*, meaning landed estates). Within these praedial servitudes there were those that applied mainly to rural land, known as 'rustic servitudes', and those that applied mainly to land in buildings in towns, known as 'urban servitudes'.

There were various sorts of urban servitudes: a right to light, to sunlight, to a view (of the sea or the mountains, for example), to drainage over someone else's land, and to the shared use of a wall supporting two adjacent properties. These types of servitudes were all concerned with town living, where properties and blocks of flats could affect their neighbours – and in Rome and other cities, three- and four-storeyed blocks of flats were quite normal.

So, if you liked plenty of light or a good view of the sea from your house, you didn't want your neighbour building a block of flats or a high wall and obstructing you. One way of avoiding that (apart from buying your neighbour's land) was making a contract with him (and probably paying him) not to build a wall; the problem was that the contract was personal, and would be enforceable only against your neighbour, so if he died or sold his land you had no rights against his heirs or purchasers, and they could build as they chose, so you would have to start all over again. The advantage of servitudes was that they 'ran with the land' – they attached to the land itself, so if you became the owner of the benefit of a servitude, you were able to enforce it against anyone who owned the land it burdened.

Because of this feature of running with the land it was usual to speak of 'dominant' and 'servient' land, and there had to be both land that benefited from, and other land that was burdened by, the servitudes. Also, since servitudes could last for ever there were rules about what types of obligations could become servitudes: there were various types of urban servitudes, but all related to activities that benefited the dominant property, usually in a town setting. An obvious one was the right to light, so you could create a servitude with your neighbours – probably by paying them – so that they did not obstruct or reduce the light coming to your house. Paul explained this:

> Where a servitude of lights is created, it is held that what is acquired is that a neighbour must not affect our lights, but if the servitude imposed is to prevent the obscuring of lights, we seem to have especially acquired the right that a neighbour shall not raise his building any higher against our will, so as to lessen the amount of light in our house. *Paul, D.8.2.4*

If your neighbour had granted you a servitude in respect of light, he would be prevented from building higher if that obstructed your light – and that servitude would similarly restrain anyone to whom he sold or gave his house. On the other hand, if you did not have such a servitude then:

> Where a man by raising his own house shuts off the lights of his neighbour, when his house is not subject to a servitude imposed upon it, no action can be brought against him. *Ulpian, D.8.2.9*

Of course since servitudes adversely affected one party and benefited another, each would want to push the definitions of the servitude, to give as little – or gain as much – as the law would allow, so normal legal principles came into play: what precisely words mean, how much they should be taken literally, what the original purpose was, and so on. Different situations were discussed by the jurists – such as when a tree is the same as a wall:

> ... I could not have acquired [freedom from a servitude] by planting a tree in that same place ... because the tree would not remain in the same condition and place as a wall would do, on account of the natural motion of a tree. *Pomponius, D.8.2.7*

Another situation was whether the obligation not to build above a certain height applied to bushes, or only to walls – unless the servitude was intended to protect the view:

> Where buildings are subject to a servitude that no portion of them shall be raised any higher, shrubs can be placed upon them above that height; but where the servitude relates to the view and the shrubs would obstruct it, this cannot be done. *Javolenus, D.8.2.12*

There was an interesting exploration of the burden of a servitude, such that it could include not demolishing a building:

> Sometimes, however, it may be said that even where a party removes or lowers a building, he still obstructs the light; if for instance, the light entered into a house by reflection or repercussion, or in some other way. *Ulpian, D.8.2.17.2*

Finally there was a fascinating exploration of the legal distinction between the right to light and the right to sunlight. Ulpian decided that it depended on where the sun shone – so was taking account of the actual value of the sunlight, rather than merely its existence – to decide the extent of a servitude:

> If anyone plants a tree so as to interfere with the light, it may equally be stated that he acts in opposition to a servitude which has been imposed; for even a tree renders the sky less plainly visible. Where, however, what is placed there does not interfere with the light, but only cuts off the rays of the sun; if this is done in a place where it was pleasant to be without it, it can be said that he has done nothing in violation of the servitude; but if he is cutting it off from a sunroom or a balcony it must be said that because he is creating shade in a place where sunshine was needed, he acts in violation of the servitude imposed. *Ulpian, D.8.2.17*

The study of Roman law

These examples are just a few of the many aspects of Roman law, from marriage and divorce, children and slaves, owning land and goods, to making a will and dealing with the estate. As with any study of law, one explores not only where the obligations or rights or liabilities are clear, but where they are not, perhaps the victim has contributed to the harm, or the intent was clear even if the form was defective. In Roman law the stories told by the jurists come to life and, however extraordinary and out of date, take you back to glimpse their times and explore their problems. Equally important, from a legal point of view one sees in Roman law the foundations of many modern legal principles – in a state that is simple, embryonic, and clear.

Reading list

JA Crook, *Law and Life of Rome, 90 BC–AD 212* (Cornell University Press, 1984).
B Nicholas, *An Introduction to Roman Law* (Oxford University Press, 1975).

3 Tort Law

Nicholas J McBride
Pembroke College, Cambridge

Introduction

Ali Baba saw 40 thieves depositing some of their loot in a cave. The mouth of the cave was sealed by a door, which would only open if you said 'Open, Sesame'. When the 40 thieves had gone away, Ali Baba went up to the door, said 'Open Sesame', and gained access to the cave. He took away some of the thieves' treasure. Meanwhile, Jack sold his cow for five beans, which grew into a beanstalk that stretched all the way into the sky. Climbing the beanstalk, he arrived in a strange land occupied by a giant. Jack entered the giant's castle and stole some of his money.

Torts are magic in the same way as Ali Baba's 'Open, Sesame' and Jack's five beans were. Torts allow you to gain access to other people's money. Suppose Vera has suffered some kind of loss as a result of Jeffrey's doing *x*. Whether Vera will be entitled to sue Jeffrey for compensation for that loss will normally depend completely on whether Jeffrey committed a *tort* in relation to Vera by doing *x*. If he didn't, then Vera will not normally be entitled to sue Jeffrey for compensation. But if he *did*, then Vera will normally be entitled to sue Jeffrey (lawyers say, 'sue Jeffrey *in tort*') for enough money to compensate her for the loss that she has suffered.

What is a tort?

So what is a tort – this magic thing that allows you to gain access to other people's money? To understand what a tort is, you first of all have to understand some quite dry points of legal terminology.

(a) Suppose that the law says that B must not beat A up and it says this in order to protect A's interests. One shorthand way lawyers have of expressing this is to say that A has a *legal right* that B not beat him up. Another way lawyers have of expressing this fact about the law is to say that B *owes* A a *legal duty* not to beat him up.

(b) So saying that A has a right that B not beat him up, and saying that B owes A a duty not to beat him up, are just two different ways of saying exactly the same thing: that the law says that B must not beat A up and it says this in order to protect A's interests. (To save words, I won't insert the word 'legal' in front of either the word 'right' or 'duty' from now on – but it should be understood that it is there.)

(c) Suppose that B *does* beat A up. In this situation we can *either* say that B has violated one of A's rights *or* we can say that B has breached a duty owed to A. It comes to exactly the same thing. A third way of expressing what has happened here is to say that B has committed a *legal wrong in relation to A*, or – more simply – that B has *wronged* A.

We are now in a much better position to understand what a tort is. Someone who commits a tort *wrongs* someone else. So B will commit a tort in relation to A if she violates one of A's rights. To put it another, exactly equivalent, way: B will commit a tort in relation to A if she breaches a duty owed to A. This explains something which puzzles a lot of students who read cases where a claimant has sued a defendant, arguing that the defendant committed a tort in relation to her. If you look at the cases, you'll find that in some of them – particularly cases which involve the defendant's beating the claimant up or imprisoning her or invading her privacy – the basis of the defendant's liability to the claimant is said to be that he violated her rights in acting as he did. However, in other cases – particularly cases which involve the defendant's carelessly harming the claimant or failing to save the claimant from harm – the basis of the defendant's liability to the claimant is said to be that he breached a duty (a *duty of care*) owed to the claimant in acting as he did. But the difference in terminology is just that – simply a difference in terminology. In all cases, the basis of the defendant's liability to the claimant is always the same: *he wronged her*.

It follows from what has just been said that if Vera wants to sue Jeffrey in tort for compensation for the loss she has suffered as a result of Jeffrey's doing x, she will have to show that Jeffrey's doing x violated her rights. To put it another – and exactly equivalent – way, Vera will have to show that Jeffrey breached a duty owed to her in doing x. A couple of cases help to make this point.

The case of *Bradford Corporation v Pickles* [1895] AC 587 concerned a landowner called Mr Pickles. Water flowing underneath his land would eventually find its way into reservoirs run by Bradford Corporation, which supplied the town of Bradford with water. Pickles intercepted the water flowing underneath his land and stopped it flowing into Bradford Corporation's waters. It is not clear why he did this. Either he wanted to sell his land and he thought that cutting off the water flowing into the reservoirs would give Bradford Corporation an incentive to buy his land. Or he wanted to get Bradford Corporation to pay him a yearly fee for allowing water to flow under his land and into its reservoirs. Either way, Pickles was hardly acting in a very public-spirited way when he did what he did. Bradford Corporation sued Pickles in tort. Their claim failed. Lord Ashbourne observed, '[Bradford Corporation] have no case unless they can show that they are entitled to the flow of water in question … ' Now, at the time *Bradford Cororation v Pickles* was decided, the law on water rights said that if water flows in undefined channels underneath A's land and flows from there onto B's land, B has no right to receive any part of that water. As the water that flowed under Pickles's land flowed in undefined channels, Bradford Corporation had no right to receive any of the water flowing under Pickles's land. So Pickles did not violate Bradford Corporation's rights when he intercepted the water flowing under his land. He therefore committed no tort in relation to Bradford Corporation by acting as he did.

The case of *Allen v Flood* [1898] AC 1 arose out of a nasty little trade dispute. A steamship called the *Sam Weller* was being repaired in a dock in Millwall by the Glengall Iron Company. Forty boilermakers were employed on a day-to-day basis to make repairs to the ironwork of the ship. These boilermakers belonged to a trade union called, very grandly, the 'Independent Society of Boiler Makers and Iron and Steel Ship Builders'. Members of this union thought that only they should be employed to do ironwork on ships. A couple of carpenters called Flood and Taylor were also employed by the Glengall Iron Company on a day-to-day basis to make repairs to the woodwork of the *Sam Weller*. Unfortunately for them, they had been employed at some point in the past by another firm – called Mills & Knight – to do ironwork on another ship. The boilermakers who were working on the *Sam Weller* found out about this. Being much attached to the principle that only boilermakers should do ironwork on ships, they were outraged by this news and summoned a representative from their union – the Allen of *Allen v Flood* – to decide what should be done. Allen went to see the managers of the Glengall Iron Company and told them that if they did not tell Flood and Taylor at the end of the day that their services were no longer required, none of the boilermakers working on the *Sam Weller* would present themselves for work the next day. Allen had the managers over a barrel: they needed the services of the boilermakers to get the *Sam Weller* repaired. So the managers did what Allen had told them to do, and told Flood and Taylor not to bother turning up to work the next day. It is not clear why Allen acted as he did. It may be that he wanted to punish Flood and Taylor for doing ironwork on another ship. Or it may be that he wanted to make an example of Flood and Taylor so as to discourage other carpenters from doing ironwork on ships. Either way, he was hardly overflowing with the milk of human kindness the day he put Flood and Taylor out of a job.

Flood and Taylor sued Allen in tort for compensation for the losses they had suffered as a result of losing their jobs working on the *Sam Weller*. However, their claims failed. They could not show that Allen had violated their rights in acting as he did. He had been perfectly entitled to say to the Glengall Iron Company, 'It's them or us – you've got to choose'. It would have been different if Flood and Taylor had had a contract with the Glengall Iron Company under which the company had undertaken to employ them until the *Sam Weller* was completely repaired. In that situation, Flood and Taylor would have had a right that Allen not persuade the Glengall Iron Company to breach its contract with Flood and Taylor. But Flood and Taylor were employed on a day-to-day basis – they had no contractual right even to be employed the next day. And as Lord Herschell observed, there is a 'chasm' between persuading A to breach his contract with B, and persuading A not to re-employ B at the end of his current contract with B. It would also have been different if the boilermakers in *Allen v Flood* had had a contract with the Glengall Iron Company under which they had undertaken to work on repairing the *Sam Weller* until it was completely repaired. In that case, it would have been unlawful for Allen to threaten the Glengall Iron Company that if they did not let Flood and Taylor go, the boilermakers would walk out. Flood and Taylor would, in that situation, have been able to establish that Allen violated their rights in acting as he did. We all have a right that other people not intentionally cause us loss using unlawful means to do so, and Allen would have violated that right of Flood and Taylor's if he had used unlawful means to procure their dismissals. However, because the boilermakers in *Allen v Flood* were employed on a day-to-day basis – just like Flood and Taylor – they were perfectly entitled not to turn up to work the next day. So Allen did nothing unlawful in threatening the Glengall Iron Company that the boilermakers would not turn up for work next day if Flood and Taylor were not let go at the end of the day.

The cases of *Bradford Corporation v Pickles* and *Allen v Flood* are of huge importance because they illustrate the most important point that any student of tort law has to understand about tort law: if A has acted in some way that has resulted in B suffering some kind of loss, B will *not* be able to sue A in tort for compensation for that loss unless A violated B's rights in acting as he did. It won't matter that A was very wicked or unpleasant in acting as he did; or that A was wholly to blame for the loss suffered by B; or that some theory indicates that it would be a good idea to make A compensate B for the loss that B has suffered. None of that matters. The only thing that matters is whether A violated B's rights in acting as he did. If he did, then B will normally be entitled to sue A in tort for compensation for the loss she has suffered. If he did not, then B will not be entitled to sue A in tort.

Liability for omissions

Another area of tort law that makes this point about tort law brutally clear is the law on liability for omissions. Suppose, for example, that I have poured myself a glass of ginger beer from out of a bottle. You are sitting nearby and spot what I have not: that there is a decomposing snail at the bottom of the bottle. You don't warn me of this. You don't say a word. You are interested to see what will happen next. I drink all of the ginger beer in my glass. Because I'm still thirsty, I reach for the ginger beer bottle and pour its remaining contents into my glass. The remains of the snail drop into the glass. I immediately start throwing up – whether because I'm sickened at the thought that some small parts of the snail might have been in the ginger beer that I drank, or because some small parts of snail *were* in the ginger beer that I drank, and they have made me ill.

Here I have suffered some physical harm from which you could have easily saved me. It wouldn't have cost you anything to warn me that there was a decomposing snail in my ginger beer bottle and had you done so, I would have come to no harm. But if I try to sue you in tort for compensation for the injury I have suffered, my claim will fail. The reason is that I had no right that you warn me of the danger I was in. To put it another – and exactly equivalent – way, you did not owe me a duty to warn me of the danger I was in. So you did me no wrong in staying silent and allowing me to drink my ginger beer.

But *why* doesn't the law say that I had a right that you save me from harm in this situation? Giving me such a right would have caused you little inconvenience and would have done me a great deal of good. So why on earth doesn't the law say that I had a right against you in this situation that you warn me of the danger I was in? The reason why in the past the law didn't recognise the existence of rights to be saved from harm in this sort of situation is pretty obvious. Up until the twentieth century, those responsible for shaping English law took the view that, for the most part, individuals should be allowed to do what they liked so long as they did no positive harm to anyone else. This *laissez-faire*

(French for 'let do') attitude was well expressed (though not endorsed) by the Victorian poet, Arthur Hugh Clough in his poem *The Last Decalogue*: 'Thou shalt not kill; but needst not strive officiously to keep alive'.

But such attitudes have long fallen out of fashion – so why does the law *nowadays* still say that there is no right to be saved from harm in the sort of situation set out above? A couple of reasons can be given why it still might make sense for the law to hold back from finding that you owed me a duty to take steps to warn me of the danger I was in.

First of all, if the law did recognise that you owed me a duty in this kind of situation, where would it stop in imposing duties on people to rescue others from harm? Would someone who was lying unconscious in the street have a right that passers-by call him an ambulance and wait with him until the ambulance arrived? Would someone who fell ill in a theatre have a right that a 'doctor in the house' give up his evening's enjoyment to treat the patient? Would a doctor who was called at home and asked to come to treat a sick child owe that child a duty to take steps to treat her illness? Would each of us have a right that the police save us from being mugged in the street? Would a beggar in the street have a right that rich people passing him by put some money in his cap? Would starving children in Africa have a right that everyone who could afford to do so donate money to relieve their suffering? The fact is that there is no natural stopping point for the law once it embarks on the course of recognising that strangers can owe each other duties to save each other from harm. So if the law recognised that I had a right that you warn me of the danger I was in, the law as a whole would be thrown into chronic uncertainty. Nobody would know when a duty to save someone else from harm would be owed, and when it would not be.

A second reason why it might not be such a good idea for the law to recognise that I had a right that you warn me of the danger I was in from the decomposing snail is illustrated by a story told about the great American golfer, Bobby Jones. During a tournament, he accidentally touched his ball with his club, and the ball moved slightly. Nobody but Jones saw that his ball had moved. Despite this, Jones drew attention to what had happened and one stroke was added to his score. When the tournament was over – with Jones losing by one stroke – Jones was congratulated on his honesty, but he brushed the congratulations off: 'You might as well congratulate a man for not robbing a bank.' It was his duty to report what had happened, and – in his eyes – he deserved no credit for doing his duty. While few of us are as honest as Bobby Jones was, we all tend to think like him, and only give people credit for doing things *above and beyond the call of duty*. If someone merely does their duty, that is no big deal in our eyes: 'It was his job – he was supposed to do what he did. What does he want – a medal?'

So if, in the situation we have been discussing, I *had* had a right that you warn me of the danger I was in and you had warned me of that danger, you would probably have earned no credit in my eyes. You would merely have done what the law required you to do. As a result, I would feel no obligation to do something for you to repay what you had done for me. Any connection we might have made as a result of your saving me from harm would be stifled at birth. We would probably part as we had met – strangers. The great virtue of the law on liability for omissions, as it stands at the moment, is that by holding back and not imposing a duty on you to save me from harm, it gives you the opportunity to earn credit in my eyes. If you take the opportunity, your doing so will create the potential for us to form some sort of connection and perhaps friendship. So the law appears to act quite coldly in refusing to recognise the existence of a duty to rescue in situations such as the one we have been discussing. However, by doing this, it leaves people space to create warm relationships between themselves based on gratuitous acts of kindness or helpfulness. Were the law to act more warmly and impose wide-ranging duties on us to rescue each other from harm, the consequence of its doing so might be to make the world a colder, more barren place.

Vicarious liability

Suppose that you have committed a tort in relation to me and I have suffered some kind of loss as a result. In this situation, I'll normally be entitled to sue you in tort for compensation for the loss that I have suffered. Now, if you were an employee of Ted's at the time you committed your tort, and you committed your tort *in the course of your employment* by Ted, Ted will be said to be *vicariously liable* for your tort, with the result that I will be entitled not only to sue you in tort for compensation for the loss I have suffered, but Ted as well. (This does not mean, of course, that I can recover double damages for the loss I have suffered – once from you, and once from Ted. If you fully compensate me for the loss I have suffered, then that will let Ted off the hook. Similarly, if Ted fully compensates me for the loss I have suffered, you won't then have to compensate me for the loss I have suffered.)

So, for example, in *Poland v John Parr & Sons* [1927] 1 KB 236, the defendants transported a waggon piled high with bags of sugar across Liverpool. The defendants employed a carter called Arthur Hall to walk alongside the waggon to make sure no one stole a bag of sugar from the waggon as it went through the streets of Liverpool. The claimant was a 12-year-old schoolboy. Being a helpful soul, he thought he would help Arthur Hall stop people stealing bags of sugar from the waggon. So he walked alongside the waggon and put a protective hand on one of the bags of sugar. Unfortunately, Hall misinterpreted the claimant's motives, and thought the claimant was trying to steal a bag of sugar from the waggon. So Hall hit the claimant, with the result that the claimant fell to the floor and the waggon rolled over his right foot, damaging it. In hitting the claimant, Hall committed a tort – the tort of *battery* (unlawful touching). The claimant sued the defendants for compensation for the injuries he had suffered as a result of Hall's battery, claiming that the defendants were vicariously liable for Hall's tort. The claimant's claim succeeded. It was held that Hall had been acting in the course of his employment by the defendants when he hit the claimant. Hall had been employed by the defendants to protect the bags of sugar on the waggon – and Hall had been trying to do precisely that when he hit the claimant. It didn't matter that when Hall hit the claimant, he was trying to do his job in a completely unreasonable and unauthorised manner. Hall was still trying to do his job when he hit the claimant, and that sufficed to establish that he was acting in the course of his employment.

So, why does the law make an employer vicariously liable for a tort that was committed by his employee if that tort was committed in the course of the employee's employment? A number of different explanations have been advanced over the years.

First, if we consider the facts of the *Poland case*, if Arthur Hall were the only person who could be sued for compensation by the claimant in *Poland*, the claimant would probably not have been able to recover very much by way of compensation for the injuries he suffered as a result of Hall's tort. Hall simply would not have had enough money to foot the bill for the claimant's injuries. Holding the defendants in *Poland* vicariously liable for Hall's tort guaranteed that the claimant could sue someone who was worth suing for compensation for his injuries. But this explanation of why there was vicarious liability in *Poland* does not work. It does not explain why the courts would *not* have held the defendants vicariously liable for Hall's tort if he had not been acting in the course of his employment. The need to provide the victim of Hall's tort with someone to sue who had 'deep pockets' would have been just as pressing whether or not Hall's tort happened to be committed in the course of his employment.

Secondly, some commentators have argued that holding employers vicariously liable for their employees' torts in cases like *Poland* helps encourage employers to take steps to ensure that the employees do not commit torts. However, this explanation does not work. If this explanation were correct, we would expect the law to say that an employer will be vicariously liable for an employee's tort if the employer could have possibly done something to stop that tort being committed. But the law does not say that.

Thirdly, it has become increasingly fashionable to explain the findings of vicarious liability in cases like *Poland* along the following lines: 'If a business operates in a way that creates a risk that I will suffer a particular kind of loss, then it is only fair that if that risk materialises and I suffer that loss, I should be able to sue that business for compensation for that loss. After all, the business gets to keep the profits that it makes from operating in the way it does; so it should also have to bear the losses that result from its operating in the way it does. If this is right, it follows that if a business employs you to work for it, and in so doing it creates a risk that you will commit a particular kind of tort in relation to me and cause me loss, then it is only fair that if that risk materialises and you commit that tort in relation to me and I suffer loss as a result, I should be able to sue the business for compensation for the loss that I have suffered. Holding the business vicariously liable for your tort allows me to sue the business for compensation for the loss I have suffered.'

However, if this explanation were correct we would expect the law to say that an employer will be vicariously liable for an employee's tort if the nature of the job the employee was employed to do gave him the opportunity to commit that tort. But the law does not say that. Suppose, for example, that in the *Poland* case, while accompanying the waggon of bags of sugar through the streets of Liverpool, Hall had seen one of his enemies standing by the side of the road. Suppose further that Hall had taken a bag of sugar from the waggon, thrown it at his enemy, and knocked him out. Hall's employers would not have been held vicariously liable for Hall's tort in this situation. Hall's tort would not have been committed in the course of his employment. He would have been engaged on a 'frolic of his own' in throwing the bag of sugar at his enemy. But if the explanation of the law on vicarious liability advanced in the previous paragraph were correct, we would expect Hall's employers to be held vicariously liable for Hall's tort in this situation. By employing Hall to escort the waggon of sugar bags through the streets of Liverpool, they created a risk that he would injure his enemy in the way he did.

Fourthly and finally, it has been argued that holding employers liable for their employees' torts in cases such as *Poland* is socially beneficial. The idea is that allowing the victim of a tort to sue the tortfeasor's employer for compensation for the losses that she has suffered via the device of vicarious liability allows those losses to be shifted onto the tortfeasor's employer. They can then be spread throughout the community. This is done in one of two ways. Either the tortfeasor's employer makes his customers pay just a little bit extra for his goods or services in order to cover the cost of paying compensation to the victim of the tort. Or the tortfeasor's employer gets his insurance company (which has promised – under a *liability insurance policy* – to cover the employer's legal liabilities) to cover the cost of compensating the victim of the tort, and the insurance company then spreads the cost of paying that compensation throughout the community by charging its customers slightly higher premiums. Either way, the law on vicarious liability works to ensure that the victim of a tort does not have to bear all the losses resulting from that tort being committed, with the result that he suffers huge disruption to his life. Instead, those losses are spread out among the community, with each of us bearing a tiny and easily borne proportion of those losses. The trouble with this explanation of the law on vicarious liability is the same problem that afflicts the first explanation that we considered above. It does not explain why employers are only held vicariously liable for torts committed by their employees if those torts were committed by their employees *in the course of their employment*. The need to spread the losses suffered by the victim of a tort committed by an employee remains exactly the same, whether or not that tort was committed in the course of the employee's employment.

The truth is that none of the traditional justifications of the law on vicarious liability provides a satisfactory explanation as to why we have a law on vicarious liability in the first place. So the law on vicarious liability seems to serve no rational purpose. It does, however, serve to keep tort lawyers in business. Were it not for the law on vicarious liability, very few tort claims would be brought in English courts. This is because in almost all tort cases, the only thing that makes it worthwhile to bring a claim for compensation is the prospect that the damages will be paid by an employer, who can usually afford to foot the bill involved in meeting the claim.

The future of tort law

It is periodically suggested by some academic commentators that the law of tort be abolished, either on the ground that it serves no useful purpose or on the ground that whatever useful purposes it does serve could be better achieved through some other mechanism.

Such commentators usually view tort law in one of two ways. Some think of tort law as an off-shoot of the criminal law. According to this view, tort law helps to ensure that our rights are not violated by imposing sanctions on people who violate those rights – the relevant sanction being a liability to pay damages to the person whose rights have been violated. People who take this view of tort law propose that it should be abolished because the person who ends up paying the compensation payable to the victim of a tort will not actually usually be the person who committed the tort. Either the tortfeasor's employer will pay, thanks to the law on vicarious liability, or the tortfeasor's liability insurer will pay. So tort law does not actually work very well to deter people from violating other people's rights. If, then, the function of tort law is to act as an off-shoot of the criminal law, it should be abolished on the ground that it does not actually perform that function anymore.

Other academic commentators take the view that the function of tort law is to ensure that those who deserve to be compensated for the fact that they have suffered a loss of some kind are able to gain compensation for that loss. Such commentators point out that tort law does a lousy job of fulfilling this function. First of all, tort law does a terrible job of delivering compensation to those who *deserve* to be compensated for some loss that they have suffered. It will protect a millionaire whose Rolls Royce has been carelessly scratched by a cyclist going to work; but it won't do anything for a baby who has been born horribly deformed because of a defect in its genetic make-up. Tort law protects the millionaire because his rights have been violated; and it does nothing for the baby because the baby's rights have not been violated. But if tort law's job is to deliver compensation to those who are most deserving of it, it is difficult to understand why tort law focuses on whether someone's rights have been violated. It is simply not the case that people whose rights have been violated are the most deserving of compensation. Secondly, tort law is an extremely expensive and inefficient vehicle for delivering compensation to people who deserve to be compensated for some loss that they have suffered. It costs a lot of time and money to determine whether a particular claimant is entitled to sue a particular defendant in tort for compensation for some loss he has suffered; it also costs a lot of money for potential defendants to protect themselves against being sued in tort for compensation by taking out liability insurance policies. And – given the perils involved in bringing a claim in tort against someone else – there is no guarantee that those who qualify for compensation under the tort law rules will actually obtain that compensation. If, then, the function of tort law is to deliver compensation to those who are most deserving of it, it seems undeniable that tort law should be scrapped and replaced by a new system that will do a better job of performing that function.

However, before we rush to condemn tort law, we should first of all examine whether the premises underlying our judgment are justified. Is it true to say that the function of tort law is to act as an off-shoot of the criminal law? This seems implausible. If the function of tort law is to impose sanctions on people who violate other people's rights, why does tort law do this by making tortfeasors pay *compensation* to the victims of their torts? Why doesn't it fine tortfeasors for what they have done, with the fines being adjusted according to the degree of a tortfeasor's fault for what he did? Alternatively, is it true to say that the function of tort law is to deliver compensation to those who are most deserving of it? Again, this seems implausible. As we have already observed, if it were the case that tort law's job was simply to deliver compensation to those who are most deserving of it, it is hard to understand why tort law simply focuses on protecting those whose rights have been violated.

So what is the function of tort law? It is submitted that *the function of tort law is to enable people to vindicate their rights in the face of those who would violate them*. If A is proposing to do something that will violate B's rights, tort law allows B to obtain an injunction, requiring A not to violate B's rights on pain of being sent to prison if he does. If A has already done something to violate B's rights, tort law allows B to sue A for damages designed to put her in as good a position as she would have been in had A respected her rights. Viewed in this light, the idea of abolishing tort law becomes faintly preposterous. Abolishing tort law would mean we could no longer take steps ourselves to vindicate our rights in the face of those who would violate them. We would instead become wholly dependent on the State, acting through the criminal law, to protect us from those who would violate our rights. So abolishing tort law would bring about a very significant and almost certainly unjustified transfer of power from the individual to the State.

Reading list

P Atiyah, *The Damages Lottery* (Oxford: Hart Publishing, 1997).
J Harr, *A Civil Action* (Random House, 1995).
NJ McBride & R Bagshaw, *Tort Law* (2nd edn, Pearson Education 2005).

4 Criminal Law

Nicholas J McBride
Pembroke College, Cambridge

Introduction

The criminal law performs two primary functions. The first – what I will call the 'core' function – is to protect our rights by punishing those who deliberately violate them. The criminal law performs this core function when it punishes murderers, rapists and thieves. All these categories of people deliberately violate other people's rights. The second function – what I will call the 'secondary' function – is to deter people from acting in ways that are contrary to the public interest. The criminal law performs this secondary function when it punishes polluters, drug dealers and public officials who act corruptly. None of these categories of people can be said to violate other people's rights; but they do act in ways that are contrary to the public interest.

The language that I've used to describe these two functions of the criminal law might be taken to suggest that the vast majority of criminal offences are concerned with protecting our rights, and that these offences are orbited by a small number of criminal offences that are concerned to deter people from acting in an anti-social way. In fact, the opposite is true. It has been estimated that there are about 8,000 different criminal offences that may be committed in England and Wales. (That number is rapidly increasing all the time – more than 700 different criminal offences were created between 1997 and 2003.) No more than 100 of those offences are concerned with protecting our rights. I'll call these offences 'rights-based' offences. All of the other criminal offences recognised in England and Wales exist to deter people from acting in ways that are contrary to the public interest. I'll call these offences 'public interest-based' offences. Despite this disparity in the number of rights-based offences and public interest-based offences, almost all of the offences that a law student will study when he or she studies 'criminal law' will be rights-based in nature. He or she will spend virtually no time looking at offences that exist to deter people from acting in ways that are contrary to the public interest.

In order to establish that a defendant has committed a rights-based offence, it has to be shown that the defendant has violated someone else's rights, and that he did so deliberately. In the language customarily used by criminal lawyers, it has to be shown that the defendant committed an *actus reus* (a wrongful act) with a *mens rea* (a wrongful mind).

In contrast, in order to establish that a defendant has committed a public interest-based offence, it will always be necessary to show that the defendant acted in a way that was contrary to the public interest, but it will almost never be necessary to show that the defendant acted deliberately. For example, suppose the law said that a company that has polluted a river will only be guilty of an offence if it polluted it deliberately. Such a rule would not do anything to encourage a company to take safety precautions to ensure it did not pollute a nearby river. It would know that if it failed to take such precautions with the result that it polluted the river, it would face no criminal punishment as the pollution was not deliberate. What if the law said that a company that has polluted a river *carelessly* will be guilty of an offence? Such a rule would almost certainly encourage our company to take some precautions to ensure that it did not pollute the river, but it would probably do no more than the bare minimum to see that it did not pollute the river. It would bet that doing no more than the bare minimum would be enough to escape being successfully prosecuted for carelessly polluting the river. The only rule which would encourage the company to do as much as it could to avoid polluting the river would be one which said that a company that has polluted a river will be guilty of an offence if it could *possibly* have done *something* to avoid polluting the river. Under this *strict liability* rule, the company would know that unless it could prove that it had done *everything possible* to avoid polluting the river, every time it polluted the river, it would face a fine. It's for this reason that most public interest-based offences do not require it to be shown that the defendant acted with any kind of *mens rea*. Instead, most public interest-based offences are strict liability in nature, holding the defendant liable unless it can be shown that the defendant did everything possible to avoid doing what the defendant did.

The meaning of intention

The most serious criminal offence recognised in English law is, of course, murder. This is a rights-based offence, protecting a person's right that others not unjustly deprive them of their life. A will commit the offence of murder if:

(a) A's actions cause another to die; and

(b) when A performed those actions he had an intent to kill; and

(c) A had no lawful justification or excuse for acting as he did.

(Note that this definition is not strictly accurate: to convict A of murder it will be enough to show that when A acted as he did, he had an intent to cause someone to suffer really serious bodily harm. However, to keep things simple this point about the law will be disregarded in the discussion below.)

So, for example, suppose that I attend a political rally carrying a gun. I intend to use the gun to kill the main speaker at the rally. A policewoman spots that I have a gun. She sidles up to me and attempts to take the gun away from me. In the ensuing struggle, the gun goes off accidentally and the policewoman is killed. Am I guilty of murder? Yes, I am. Running through each of the elements that have to be made out before I can be found guilty of murder:

(a) my bringing a gun to the rally caused the policewoman to die – had I not brought the gun to the rally, she would not have died;

(b) when I took the gun to the rally, I intended to kill the main speaker at the rally (note that it does not have to be shown that I intended to kill the very person who died as a result of my actions);

(c) I had no lawful justification or excuse for bringing the gun to the rally.

Now, let's consider a different case. I need to raise a lot of money very urgently. I own a passenger plane that is insured for £20m. I plant a bomb on the plane just before it is due to take off. My idea is that when the bomb goes off, the plane will blow up and I will be able to collect the insurance on the plane. The bomb explodes 30 minutes after the plane takes off, and all the passengers and crew on the plane are killed. Am I guilty of murder? There is no doubt that my action in planting a bomb on the plane has caused the deaths of the passengers and the crew, and there is equally no doubt that I had no justification or excuse for doing what I did. The real difficulty is in establishing that I had the *mens rea* for murder. When I planted the bomb, can I say that I intended to kill someone?

In principle, the answer is 'No'. I intend to bring about a certain outcome if it is my aim or purpose to bring about that outcome. When I planted the bomb, my *aim* or *purpose* was *not* to kill anyone. Suppose that in the case we are considering, by some miracle no one was killed or seriously injured as a result of the plane blowing up. In such a case, would I have snapped my fingers and thought, 'Confound it! My plans didn't work out! The plane was blown up but no one was killed! That's not what I wanted!' Of course I wouldn't have. I probably would have thought, 'Thank goodness no one was killed. Now I can collect the insurance money on my plane with a clear conscience.' So it was not my aim or purpose to kill anyone when I planted the bomb. It follows that, in principle, I should be acquitted of murder. When I planted the bomb I did not have an intent to kill.

However, this would not be regarded by most people as a satisfactory result. In this case, I have exhibited a callous disregard for the rights of the passengers and crew not to be unjustly deprived of their lives. As a result, most people would regard me as being *just as bad* as someone who acts with a clear intention to kill, such as an assassin. If I am just as bad as an assassin, people will think that I should be convicted of murder, just like the assassin. To achieve this result, the courts have twisted the definition of when someone can be said to have had an intent to kill. The courts say that a defendant will have had an intent to kill if: (1) he or she acted with the aim or purpose of killing someone; *or* (2) when he or she acted, he or she knew that it was virtually certain that someone would be killed as a result of his or her actions. Adopting this definition allows me to be convicted of murder in the case we are considering. When I planted the bomb on the plane I knew it was *virtually certain* that the passengers and crew on the plane would be killed as a result – so under the courts' definition of intention I can be said to have had an intent to kill when I planted the bomb on the plane. And if I can be said to have had an intent to kill, then I am guilty of murder.

A good result? In this particular case, yes. However, while it is very common for the courts to twist legal rules – redefining their terms – in order to achieve the results that they want to achieve in particular cases, manipulating legal rules in this way is rarely a good idea in the long run. Consider whether the offence of murder has been committed in the following situation. You and I are mountaineering. We are attached by a rope. You are below me on the mountain. You lose your footing on the mountain and slip into a deep crevasse. I manage to keep my place on the mountain, but we are now stuck. The only thing stopping you from falling to your death is the rope that attaches you to me. I don't have the strength to haul you out of the crevasse, and you cannot get any kind of footing that would allow you to climb out of the crevasse. Night is approaching and we will both freeze on the mountain if we remain where we are. In the end I decide to cut the rope that attaches you to me: it's better that one of us (that is, you) should die than that we should both die. I cut the rope and you fall to your death. Am I guilty of murder? My cutting the rope undoubtedly caused your death. But when I cut the rope, did I intend to kill you? If we define 'intention' in the way it is normally defined, I did not intend to kill you. When I cut the rope it was not my aim or purpose to kill you. Had you by some miracle survived your fall, I would have been delighted. I would not have snapped my fingers and thought, 'Confound it! I thought I'd finished you off! Now I'm going to have to find some other way of getting rid of you!' However, according to the courts' definition of intention, I *did* have an intent to kill in this situation: while my aim or purpose in cutting the rope may not have been to kill you, I did know at the time I cut the rope that it was virtually certain that you would die as a result.

Would it be a good result to find me guilty of murder? Of course not. I don't exhibit anything like the callous disregard for people's rights to life that is shown by either the assassin or by the plane bomber in the case we were considering above. But if my actions caused your death, and I had an intent to kill you when I performed those actions, then I will be guilty of murder unless the courts recognise that I had a lawful justification or excuse for my actions. So, what sort of justification or excuse can I rely on in this situation? The most obvious one is a defence of *necessity*: 'The circumstances meant that I did the right thing when I cut the rope. If I had not cut the rope, both of us would have died. By cutting the rope, I ensured that at least one of us (that is, me) survived.'

So, problem solved. We can recognise a defence of necessity in this case, and thereby ensure that I am not convicted of murder. But if we do that, what does that imply for the following case? Bob is wheeled into Dr Strange's hospital with a rare blood condition that threatens to kill him in the next two hours. The only cure is to give Bob a complete blood transfusion, replacing all of his blood with new blood. Unfortunately, there are no blood bags available of the same blood type as Bob's. Another patient, Eric, is in Dr Strange's hospital. He suffers from cancer. His cancer is incurable and it is predicted that he probably only has six more weeks to live. Eric's blood type is the same as Bob's. Dr Strange orders that Eric be sedated, and all his blood drained from his body and given to Bob. Eric dies as a result of this treatment. Is Dr Strange guilty of murder? He has the *actus reus* and *mens rea* of murder – but can he take advantage of a defence of necessity here to establish that he had a lawful justification or excuse for doing what he did? If we allow a defence of necessity in the mountaineering case set out above, it is hard to see why we would not allow one here. Why could Dr Strange not argue, 'The circumstances meant I did the right thing when I drained Eric's blood from his body. If I had not done that, both Bob (immediately) and Eric (eventually) would have died. By draining Eric's blood from his body, I ensured that at least one of them (that is, Bob) survived.'

I think most people would be unhappy if Dr Strange were allowed to escape a murder charge in this situation by relying on a defence of necessity. But it would seem that we *have* to allow him such a defence if we allow such a defence to be raised in the mountaineering case. Of course, we only have to allow such a defence to be raised in the mountaineering case because the courts have ruled that a defendant will be held to have had an intent to kill if he acted as he did knowing that death was a virtually certain consequence of his actions. If we got rid of that rule and returned to the idea that you can only be said to intend the consequences of your actions if it was your aim or purpose to produce those consequences, then we could find that there was no murder in the mountaineering case because there was no intent to kill. However, if we find there was no intent to kill in the mountaineering case, then we would have to find there was no intent to kill and therefore no murder in the plane bomber case and in Dr Strange's case as well. (Dr Strange could argue that it was not his aim or purpose to kill Eric when he drained Eric of his blood – had Eric by some miracle survived without his blood, he would have been delighted.)

We seem to be stuck. If we adopt a strict line on when someone can be said to have had an intent to kill, some defendants who deserve to be convicted of murder will be acquitted. If we relax the definition of when someone can be said to have had an intent to kill – and say that you will have an intent to kill if you act knowing that death is a virtually certain consequence of your actions – then you will bring within the scope of the law of murder people who do not deserve to be convicted of murder. The only way of saving them from being convicted of murder will be to provide them with defences to being charged with murder; which defences may then be taken advantage of by people who *do* deserve to be convicted of murder.

Is there any way out of this mess? One way would be to redefine when someone is guilty of murder and say that someone will commit the crime of murder if he acts in a way that causes another's death and at the time he acted he exhibited a callous disregard for other people's rights not to be unjustly deprived of their lives. Under this rule, the plane bomber and Dr Strange would be convicted of murder. Both exhibited a callous disregard for other people's rights to life in acting as they did. In contrast, I would be acquitted of murder for cutting the rope in the mountaineering case set out above. In that case, I did not exhibit a callous disregard for your right to life in acting as I did.

Morality and the criminal law

The above discussion shows the important role played by considerations of morality in developing the criminal law. The perception that a particular person is *just as bad* as someone who is clearly guilty of murder leads the courts to reshape the rules on when someone can be found to have an intent to kill. And when those rules operate in such a way as to threaten that a defendant who does *not deserve* to be convicted of murder will be convicted, the courts respond to that threat by reshaping the law on when someone can be said to have had a lawful justification or excuse for acting as he did, and provide that someone with a defence.

Should considerations of morality play an even greater role in the development of the criminal law? Should the criminal law take on a third function – that of encouraging people to act morally, by punishing them for acting immorally? The Victorian philosopher, John Stuart Mill thought that it should not. In his book *On Liberty* (published in 1859), he argued:

> [T]he only purpose for which power can be rightfully exercised over any member of a civilised community, against his will, is to prevent harm to others. His own good, either physical or moral, is not sufficient warrant. He cannot rightfully be compelled to do or forbear because it will be better for him to do so, because it will make him happier, because, in the opinion of others, to do so would be wise or even right …

The modern consensus is that the criminal law should observe Mill's 'harm principle', so that conduct should only be criminalised if it violates other people's rights or if it harms the public interest. The fact that acting in a particular way is immoral does not give us sufficient reason to make it a criminal offence to act in that way. Having said that, two fairly recent cases may be interpreted as breaking with this consensus.

R v Brown

In *R v Brown* [1994] 1 AC 212, a group of sado-masochists were charged with committing offences under ss 20 and 47 of the Offences Against the Person Act 1861. (Someone will commit an offence under s 20 if he maliciously wounds or inflicts grievous bodily harm on another. Someone will commit an offence under s 47 if he commits an assault on another person that occasions actual bodily harm.) The defendants deliberately inflicted pain on each other by doing such things as driving nails into each other's bodies; burning each other with candles; and cutting each other with knives. Each of the defendants fully consented to having these things done to them.

The House of Lords had to decide whether the defendants had committed offences under the 1861 Act in acting as they had. By a majority of three to two, the House of Lords decided that they had. Some of the judgments of the majority give the impression that they thought the defendants should be punished because they had acted immorally. Lord Templeman remarked, 'Pleasure derived from the infliction of pain is an evil thing. Cruelty is uncivilised.' Lord Lowry argued that no exemption from the 1861 Act should be made for people who 'wish to satisfy a perverted and depraved sexual desire'. In contrast, Lord Mustill argued in dissent that the defendants should not be convicted. He based himself on Mill's harm principle: '[Questions as to whether the activities of the members of the group were right or wrong] are questions of private morality; … the standards by which they fall to be judged are not those of the criminal law; … if these standards are to be upheld the individual must enforce them upon himself … or have them enforced against him by moral pressures exerted by whatever … community to whose ethical ideals he responds.'

A couple of arguments might be made in favour of the view that convicting the defendants in *Brown* did not violate Mill's harm principle. Neither of them are convincing.

First, *violation of rights*. At first sight, it seems that the activities in *Brown* did not violate the rights of those who were the object of those activities. Rights can almost always be waived. For example, I have a right that you do not smash up my car. But if I invite you to smash up my car and you do so, you will not have violated my rights. I will have waived my right that you do not smash up my car.

In a similar way, it can be argued that each of the sado-masochists in *Brown* waived their rights not to be physically harmed by the other sado-masochists; so whenever a particular defendant physically harmed a fellow sado-masochist, he did not violate that sado-masochist's rights. However, this argument overlooks the fact that some rights are *inalienable*. They cannot be waived. It is arguable that one's right not to be treated in a cruel and inhumane manner is one such right. If this is correct, then it can be argued that every time one of the sado-masochists in *Brown* was injured by a fellow sado-masochist, his rights *were* violated. So punishing the defendants in *Brown* fulfilled the criminal law's core function – that of protecting our rights by punishing those who deliberately violate them.

The weakness in this argument is that it is not clear why one's right not to be treated in a cruel and inhumane manner should be inalienable. Nor is it clear why the criminal law should go out of its way to protect rights that the right-holders are plainly not interested in having.

Secondly, *the public interest*. The majority in *Brown* placed a good deal of stress on the harm that might be done to the public interest if activities such as those that went on in *Brown* were allowed to continue. Lord Jauncey of Tullichettle pointed out, 'it would appear to be good luck rather than good judgment that ... prevented serious injury occurring [in this case]. Wounds can easily become septic if not properly treated, the free flow of blood from a person who is HIV positive or who has Aids can infect another ... '. Underlying this statement is a concern that if someone was seriously injured as a result of engaging in sado-masochistic activities, the public would have to pick up the tab for treating his injuries on the National Health Service (NHS). It follows that engaging in sado-masochistic activities is contrary to the public interest, and in punishing those who engage in such activities, the criminal law is fulfilling its secondary function – that of deterring people from acting in ways that are contrary to the public interest.

If this argument in favour of the decision in *Brown* were correct, then many other activities could justifiably be criminalised. As Lord Mustill pointed out in *Brown*, the same argument could be used to justify criminalising homosexual relations among men, as this is a principal cause of the spread of HIV and Aids in the UK. It could also be used to justify making criminals of people who spend their spare time skateboarding or mountain-climbing or smoking cigarettes in private. In effect, if this argument in favour of criminalising the activities in *Brown* were accepted, the existence of the NHS in the UK would make it justifiable to deprive people of the freedom to decide what to do with their own bodies. The socialisation of heath care in the UK would have the effect of justifying the socialisation of people's bodies. This cannot be right. The fact that the State has created a national health care system cannot be invoked by the State as a reason for taking away from people liberties that they would have enjoyed in the absence of such a health care system.

So it seems that the House of Lords decision in *Brown did* violate Mill's harm principle. In *Brown*, the criminal law was used to force people to act morally – no other explanation of the case makes sense.

R v Hinks

In *R v Hinks* [2001] 2 AC 241, a 38-year-old called Karen Hinks befriended a 53-year-old man called John Dolphin. Dolphin was a naïve, trusting man of limited intelligence. Hinks became his principal carer. Dolphin had substantial savings and money inherited from his father in a building society account. From April to November 1996, Hinks and Dolphin went to Dolphin's building society virtually every day. Dolphin would withdraw £300 each time, and then give the money to Hinks. By the end of the six months, Dolphin had given Hinks approximately £60,000.

Hinks was convicted of theft and the House of Lords upheld her conviction, by a three to two majority. The majority found that all the elements of the offence of theft were present in Hinks's case. A defendant will commit the offence of theft if he dishonestly appropriates property belonging to another with an intention permanently to deprive that other of that property. It was found that when Hinks accepted Dolphin's money, she had appropriated property belonging to Dolphin. It was further found that Hinks had acted dishonestly in accepting Dolphin's money and that when she accepted that money, she had an intent permanently to deprive Dolphin of that money.

On the facts of *Hinks*, the decision to convict Hinks of theft was unobjectionable. The law grants people of limited intelligence a right that other people not take advantage of their weakness, and will set aside any gifts or transactions that are the product of a violation of that right on the ground that the gifts or transactions are 'unconscionable'. So Dolphin had a right that Hinks not exploit his limited intelligence, and Hinks violated that right when she prevailed upon him to give her £60,000. So punishing Hinks for theft did not breach Mill's harm principle: Hinks was straightforwardly punished for deliberately violating Dolphin's rights.

However, the real danger of the decision in *Hinks* is that it opens the door to people being convicted for theft *whenever* they dishonestly accept a gift or act dishonestly in buying something. For example, consider the following two cases.

> (1) Freddie is in love with Linda. Linda does not care for Freddie, but she does not make her true feelings clear to Freddie because he lavishes so much attention and, more importantly, so many gifts on her. On Linda's 21st birthday, Freddie gives Linda a diamond necklace, worth £20,000.

> (2) Howard walks into Bill's antique shop where a painting is on sale for £50. Howard recognises that the painting is by Rembrandt, and is in fact worth £2m. Howard gives Bill £50 for the painting on the spot and walks out of the shop with it.

If we find that Linda's and Howard's conduct in these situations was 'dishonest' then the decision in *Hinks* suggests that each of them will be guilty of theft. However, neither of them has violated anyone's rights in acting as they did. The law does not confer on Freddie a right that Linda not take advantage of his infatuation for her. The law says that in affairs of the heart, Freddie has to look after himself. If Linda makes a fool of him, then that is his lookout. Similarly, the law does not confer a right on Bill that Howard not take advantage of Bill's ignorance of the true value of his goods to snap up a bargain for himself. If Bill ends up selling a painting to Howard for far less than it is actually worth, then that is his lookout.

So if Linda and Howard are convicted of theft in the above situations, even though they did not violate anyone's rights, the law will in effect punish them simply for acting 'dishonestly'. In so doing, the law will violate Mill's harm principle, under which the mere fact that someone's conduct is immoral (or, here, 'dishonest') is not enough to justify criminalising it.

Evaluating Mill's harm principle

Of course, the fact that John Stuart Mill thought that the criminal law should not be used to force people to act morally does *not* establish that the criminal law should not be used in this way. Why shouldn't the criminal law be used to force people to act morally? Three reasons can be given.

First, it is not clear what the point is of *forcing* someone to act morally. Let's assume that it is immoral for Wendy to cheat on her husband by sleeping with Ethan. Threatening to punish Wendy if she sleeps with Ethan may deter her from cheating on her husband, but forcing Wendy not to cheat on her husband will not make her into a better or wiser person. Instead, it will simply make her feel cowed and resentful.

Secondly, in today's society there is no consensus on what sort of behaviour is moral and what sort of behaviour is immoral, particularly in the areas of sexual activity and drug taking. There is not even a consensus on how to resolve disagreements over what sort of conduct is moral or immoral. Given this, the idea of using the criminal law to force people to act morally is particularly problematic. Whose view of what is moral and immoral should govern? The Church's? The State's?

Thirdly, criminalising behaviour that is commonly believed to be immoral may have the effect of entrenching mistaken moral beliefs. For example, in parts of the United States it was at one time thought that it was immoral for a black man and a white woman to go out with each other. Had such behaviour been criminalised in the United States, it would have been very hard to challenge this thoroughly evil belief. Indeed, the lack of examples of black men and white women going out with each other that would have been produced by criminalising such behaviour would have encouraged people to think that there was indeed something wrong, or unnatural, in black men and white women going out with each other.

In light of these arguments, it seems that Mill was right. The criminal law should not play a role in forcing people to act morally, but should instead confine itself to performing the two functions identified at the start of this chapter – that of punishing people who deliberately violate other people's rights, and that of deterring people from acting in ways that are contrary to the public interest.

Reading list

CMV Clarkson, *Understanding Criminal Law*, (4th edn, London: Sweet & Maxwell, 2005).

J Herring, *Criminal Law*, (4th edn, Basingstoke: Palgrave Macmillan, 2005).

J Herring, *Text, Cases and Materials on Criminal Law* (Oxford: Oxford University Press, 2004).

HLA Hart, *Law, Liberty and Morality* (1963).

Lord Devlin, *The Enforcement of Morals* (Oxford: Oxford University Press, 1959).

5   Land Law

Dr Neil Jones
Magdalene College, Cambridge

Land law was one of the earliest aspects of English law to develop as a system of rules and principles: Sir Thomas Littleton's *New Tenures*, the first law book printed in England and the first textbook on English land law, was published in the 1480s, centuries before there were textbooks on other areas. Land law was precocious because of land-holding's importance in the Middle Ages as a basis for political power and the ordering of society, and because of land's economic importance: it is a finite resource, and before the Industrial Revolution and the development of modern financial markets was a key form of wealth.

The political and economic role of land-holding is less dominant in the modern world, but human life is inevitably a continuous interaction with land, and we are constantly engaged with aspects of land law. From going into a restaurant for a meal or into a cinema to see a film, to renting a cottage for a holiday or buying a house with mortgage finance, land law accompanies us at every turn, playing a central role in the functioning of society.

Classification of interests

While going into a cinema to see a film and buying a house both involve interactions with land, the two activities are clearly very different. The difference which is of particular concern to land lawyers lies in the rights which the cinema-goer and the house-buyer have in respect of the land; clearly these rights are not the same. Just as there is a variety of possible interactions with land, so there is a variety of possible rights in respect of land, and since these rights do not all have the same characteristics, land law is concerned to classify them.

At a fundamental level, rights in respect of land are classified as to whether they are property rights or matters of personal obligation. (Of course there may also be interactions with land which confer no rights at all: a child allowed into a neighbour's garden to recover a ball is not trespassing, but could lawfully be told to leave at any moment.) The nature of property rights is much debated, but we may say among other things that a property right in respect of land is likely to be protected by the law from being removed; is likely to entitle the owner of the right to exclude other people (though not necessarily all other people); is likely to entitle the owner of the right to decide how to use, or whether to use, the land; and is likely to be capable of being asserted against the world at large (or most of it), and not only against the person who granted the right. The last point is particularly important: if in return for payment I let you stay with me as my lodger you will not have a property right in my house. You will have the benefit of a contract, an obligation binding me, but if I sell the house you will be unable to continue to live in it after the sale. In contrast, if I grant you a lease of my house, and then sell the house, you have a property right and may be able to insist on continuing to live in it after the sale.

Another important classification of rights in respect of land is as to whether they are legal or equitable, a distinction which is peculiarly characteristic of English law, derived from the fact that before the 1870s there were two sets of courts – the courts of common law and the courts of equity. The courts of common law were the older of the two, the first to become established as medieval kings delegated their power to do justice. The courts of equity grew up later as complaints were made to the king in situations in which the common law courts failed to provide a remedy, and the king a second time delegated his power to do justice. A good example of the distinction between law and equity is provided by *trusts*. If A transferred land to B on the understanding that B would hold it for the benefit of C, B would be recognised by the courts of common law as the owner of the land. But this told only part of the story: in a sense B *was* the owner of the land, but having received it on the understanding that he would hold it for the benefit of C, justice would not be done if B were allowed to enjoy the land for himself. So the courts of equity, building upon B's ownership as recognised by the courts of common law, insisted that B exercise that ownership for the benefit of C. B was the owner at law, but was owner as trustee for C who, as the beneficiary of the trust, had a right to the land *in equity*. Trusts are very important in land law, for example in recognising the rights of those who contribute to the purchase of land but whose names are left out of the ownership documents. They are considered in more detail in Chapter 6, the chapter on equity.

A third possible classification of rights in respect of land is in terms of rights which involve possession of land, and rights which do not. The house owner (or the tenant paying rent to the house owner) is entitled to possession of the land, and full enjoyment of it. But there are also property rights in respect of land which do not give possession or full enjoyment. We have seen one right of this type already: the mortgage lender is not expected to have possession of the land or full enjoyment of it, though if repayments are not kept up the lender may take possession and sell the land to recover the loan. Other rights in respect of land will never give possession or full enjoyment. A good example is a right of way. If A buys land in B's back garden on which to build a house, A's house may be useless unless he has a right of way across the land which A still owns so as to reach the street. B's right of way does not entitle him to possession or full enjoyment of A's land, but is nevertheless a valuable property right.

Co-ordination of rights

Land law is concerned not only with the classification of rights in land, but also with their co-ordination: a number of people may have, or claim, rights in respect of a piece of land which are potentially conflicting, and it is a function of the law to resolve these conflicts.

Some questions of co-ordination arise between people with current rights in the land. If two people jointly own a field and one of them cuts the grass and makes hay which he sells, can the other claim part of the proceeds of sale? Or if the mortgage lender repossesses a house, how careful does he have to be in selling the house to get a price which leaves a surplus for the borrower after the loan has been recovered?

Other questions of co-ordination arise between existing rights and newly created rights. Take a husband, the sole legal owner of a house, but in equity holding it upon trust partly for his wife, who secretly grants a mortgage over the house to a lender. May the wife, when the lender seeks to repossess and sell the house, claim that her equitable interest in the house is unaffected by the mortgage and so prevent a repossession?

Questions of co-ordination between existing and newly granted rights, such as that above, are at the heart of land law. There is a strong argument that the wife's equitable interest in the house should not be affected by the mortgage: she knew nothing about it, and the loan was paid entirely to her husband. But on the other hand the husband misled the lender, pretending that only he had rights in the house, and if lenders are too easily burdened by the rights of others, such as the wife, they may be less willing to lend on affordable terms. It is a question for land law to strike a balance between conflicting priorities such as these.

There are a number of ways in which land law has sought to strike such a balance. One mechanism is the establishment of a closed list of possible property rights in land: the law provides a finite number of pigeonholes into which rights in relation to land must fit if they are to be recognised as property rights. Since only property rights may be asserted against the world at large, this limitation means that someone thinking of buying land has a clear idea of what rights in the land may be capable of affecting him. New pigeonholes have from time to time been added: in the nineteenth century one was added for restrictive covenants, allowing a landowner to obtain a property right to prevent specified activities on neighbouring land, for example building, or conducting a business. In the second half of the twentieth century there was an attempt to add a new pigeonhole for contractual licences (the type of interest which lodgers typically have), but this has so far failed.

Another mechanism is the imposition of rules concerning the documentation necessary for the creation of property rights, which are referred to as rules of formality. For example, if I want to grant you a 10-year lease of my house I need to use a deed, a formal document bearing my witnessed signature; if I try to grant you the lease orally without any writing you will get nothing. Formality requirements make subsequent proof of the grant of the right easier; they tend to prevent people creating property rights without careful thought; and they help to clarify what type of property right has been created. But formality cannot be insisted upon in all cases: if A owns a house, and B moves in – being told by A that the house is as much his as it is hers – and B then spends money improving the house, no formality has been used, but it may nevertheless be impossible to deny B a property right.

A third mechanism is registration, which has now become a dominant theme of English land law, with the aim that before a purchaser buys land he will be able to discover all the registered property rights affecting the land, and can buy safe in the knowledge that any other property rights affecting the land are unregistered and cannot affect him. The theory is clear, but the practice is more difficult. What about the person with a property right who fails to register it, perhaps because he does not know that registration is required, or perhaps because he simply does not realise that he has a property right to begin with?

Some examples

Property, possession, and human rights

Most people in possession of land are not trespassers, and since the likelihood of trespassers is small it is a good working assumption that people in possession of land have a right to be there. This is the pragmatic view which English land law has always taken: possession of land is evidence of a right to that land. But what if A is the owner of land, with documents to prove it, and while A is away B moves onto the land and takes possession? English land law's pragmatic assumption that possession is evidence of a right suggests that B is the owner; but A has documents to prove that he is the owner. It would not be desirable for B to be able to put an end to A's ownership simply by wrongfully taking possession of the land, but it remains a useful working assumption that possession is evidence of a right, and B has possession.

English land law's answer to this conundrum is that A and B both have a right to the land, but that A's right is relatively better than B's: if A claims the land B cannot resist, but as against anyone else B may rely upon his possession as evidence of a right. Can A's right be better than B's for ever? Suppose A has no current use for the land, and leaves it lying empty. If B moves in, and uses the land for many years, surely there should come a time when A can no longer reclaim the land from B? English land law provides for this by the doctrine of adverse possession: if B retains possession for 12 years, A's claim to the land is extinguished.

In *Buckinghamshire County Council v Moran* [1990] Ch 623 the council were the owners of a plot of land in Chenies Avenue, Amersham, having bought it in 1955 in connection with a proposed diversion of the A404 road. It was expected that road construction would not occur for many years, and in the meantime the council had no use for the land. Mr Moran bought a house next door to the plot in 1971. He knew that the council owned the plot and that they had plans to use it for road building. The council had built a fence to separate the plot from Chenies Avenue, and Mr Moran put a lock on the gate in the fence and kept the key. He used the plot as an extension to his garden. The council knew about this, but took no action until 1985, when they began court proceedings to evict Mr Moran. In response Mr Moran relied upon the doctrine of adverse possession, claiming that he had been in adverse possession for 12 years and that therefore the council's right to the land had been extinguished by the relevant statute, the Limitation Act 1980.

In the High Court Mr Justice Hoffman decided in favour of Mr Moran; the council appealed to the Court of Appeal. The council's main argument was that following the case of *Leigh v Jack* (1879) 5 Ex D 264 it was a rule of law that adverse possession could not be established unless the supposed adverse possessor (the 'squatter') had done things on the land which were inconsistent with the owner's future plans for the land. Using the plot as

49

a garden was not inconsistent with its future use for road building, and therefore, the council argued, Mr Moran had not established adverse possession.

The Court of Appeal disagreed, and decided for Mr Moran. It was, said Lord Justice Slade:

> too broad a proposition to suggest that an owner who retains a piece of land with a view to its utilisation for a specific purpose in future can never be treated as dispossessed, however firm and obvious the intention to dispossess, and however drastic the acts of dispossession of the person seeking to dispossess him may be.

If the squatter knew of the owner's intended future use (as Mr Moran did), the court would be likely to require 'very clear evidence before it can be satisfied that the squatter who claims a possessory title has not only established factual possession of the land, but also the requisite intention to exclude the world at large, including the owner', but if such evidence was present, adverse possession could be established despite the absence of acts inconsistent with the owner's future plans. On the facts Mr Moran had put a lock on the gate in the fence and had kept the key. He had thereby established both factual possession and a clear intention to possess the land. Mr Moran having been present on this basis for 12 years, the council's ownership had been extinguished and Mr Moran could remain.

The Court of Appeal's rejection of the rule in *Leigh v Jack* was subsequently affirmed by the House of Lords in *JA Pye (Oxford) Ltd v Graham* [2003] 1 AC 419. This seemed to settle the law. But there was a further difficulty. The Human Rights Act 1998, which gives effect in English law to the European Convention on Human Rights (ECHR), came into force in October 2000. The ECHR includes in Art 1 of Protocol 1 the provision that:

> Every natural or legal person is entitled to the peaceful enjoyment of his possessions. No one shall be deprived of his possessions except in the public interest and subject to the conditions provided for by law and by the general principles of international law.

> The preceding provisions shall not, however, in any way impair the right of a State to enforce such laws as it deems necessary to control the use of property in accordance with the general interest or to secure the payment of taxes or other contributions or penalties.

How does this provision against deprivation of possessions fit with the doctrine of adverse possession as apparently settled in *Buckinghamshire County Council v Moran* and *JA Pye Ltd v Graham*? Does the operation of the doctrine give rise to a deprivation of possessions within the meaning of the Convention? And, if so, can it nevertheless be justified in the public interest?

The point arose in *Beaulane Properties Ltd v Palmer* [2006] Ch 79, on facts similar to those in *Buckinghamshire County Council v Moran*. Beaulane Properties Ltd owned a field in Harlington, near Heathrow Airport. The field was in the Green Belt, and since Beaulane Properties Ltd had been unable to obtain planning permission to develop it, it was left unused. In 1986 Mr Palmer, without permission, began to use the field to graze livestock. He repaired the fences, locked the gate, and began to charge other people to graze their livestock too. In 2003, relying upon adverse possession, Mr Palmer applied to the Land Registry to be registered as the owner of the field, which prompted the litigation.

Nicholas Strauss QC, sitting as a deputy High Court judge, decided that, apart from questions of human rights, Mr Palmer had successfully established ownership of the field by adverse possession. But he went on to consider whether this was compatible with the Human Rights Act 1998 and the ECHR. His conclusion was that it was not. First of all, it was necessary to consider whether the operation of the English law of adverse possession in the case gave rise to a deprivation of possessions. Mr Strauss concluded that it did: it could not be said, for example, that since the doctrine of adverse possession was part of English law, Beaulane Properties Ltd's ownership of the field had always been subject to the possibility of adverse possession, with the result that the operation of adverse possession did not deprive it of anything. Having established that there was a deprivation of possessions it was then necessary to consider whether the deprivation could be justified in the public interest. Mr Strauss QC concluded that it could not. The land in question was land of registered title, that is, ownership of it could be proved by reference to an entry in the central Land Register, and would not have to be proved in the old-fashioned way by production of title deeds. In land where title was not registered, the doctrine of adverse possession might operate in the public interest since it would, for example, enable a person whose title deeds had been stolen to demonstrate ownership on the basis of long possession. But where title to land was registered such arguments would not apply: ownership could always be demonstrated by reference to the Register. In some cases, such as in detailed disputes about boundaries, the doctrine of adverse possession might operate in the public interest even in land of registered title, but in most cases, including the present, there would be no sufficient public interest justification. The decision in *Buckinghamshire County Council v Moran* meant that a land owner might unjustifiably lose his land simply through inadvertence: land owners who did not know the law, and who had no present use for their land, might well turn a blind eye to someone like Mr Palmer, who was doing no harm, not realising that if they did so for too long they could end up being deprived of a valuable asset, and by a person who might be a deliberate trespasser: 'Beaulane's lack of vigilance, if that is what it is, does not merit the loss of the land and nothing Mr Palmer has done justifies his acquisition of it without payment'.

This being so, Mr Strauss QC held that the English law of adverse possession, as understood at the time of the case, was incompatible with the ECHR where title to land was registered. In such circumstances, under s 3 of the Human Rights Act 1998, English courts are directed, if possible, to interpret relevant legislation in a way 'which is compatible with the Convention rights'. Mr Strauss QC decided that this was possible: the relevant statute in this case, the Land Registration Act 1925, referred to 'adverse possession' but did not define it: the definition was a matter of case law, including *Buckinghamshire County Council v Moran*, as approved in *JA Pye Ltd v Graham*. Mr Strauss QC saw the cause of the incompatibility between the English law of adverse possession and the ECHR as being the decision in these two cases that the rule in *Leigh v Jack* was not good law. Since the squatter therefore need not act inconsistently with the owner's future plans, the owner could lose his land inadvertently. The answer, therefore, was to interpret 'adverse possession' as having the meaning which it had had in *Leigh v Jack*: adverse possession of land left unused would require acts inconsistent with the owner's future plans. Mr Palmer had done no such acts, and his claim to the field by adverse possession therefore failed.

This was a remarkable decision, showing the capacity of the ECHR to affect English land law (though the House of Lords has since made it clear that lower courts cannot use human rights grounds to overturn the decisions of higher courts). The decision in *Beaulane Properties Ltd v Palmer* was given in March 2005. In November 2005, following an application to it by JA Pye (Oxford) Ltd, the European Court of Human Rights gave its opinion on the human rights aspect of *JA Pye v Graham*, which the House of Lords had not considered because the facts in that case had arisen before the Human Rights Act 1998 came into force (*JA Pye (Oxford) Ltd v UK*, Application No 44302/02). By the narrowest of margins, four votes to three, the European Court of Human Rights held that the operation of the English law of adverse possession in favour of the squatter in that case amounted to a violation of Art 1 of Protocol 1 of the ECHR, imposing on the owner 'an individual and excessive burden [which] upset the fair balance between the demands of the public interest on the one hand and the applicants' right to the peaceful enjoyment of their possessions on the other', with the result that the UK Government could be required to pay compensation to Pye. In contrast, the minority took the view that:

> The real 'fault' in this case, if there has been any, lies with the applicant companies, rather than the Government ... Possession (ownership) carries not only rights but also and always some duties ... The duty in this particular case – to do no more than begin an action for repossession within 12 years – cannot be regarded as excessive or unreasonable.

The decision of the European Court of Human Rights in *JA Pye Ltd v Graham* (now under appeal to a Grand Chamber of the Court) does not itself change English law, but under s 2 of the Human Rights Act 1998 English courts are directed to take into account the decisions of the European Court of Human Rights. The fate of the view of adverse possession taken in *Buckinghamshire County Council v Moran* and *JA Pye Ltd v Graham* remains to be seen. In the meantime, under the Land Registration Act 2002, which came into force in October 2003, ownership of land of registered title by adverse possession will in future be very much more difficult to establish. The doctrine will apply only in a narrow range of circumstances, and the squatter will not be able to become registered as the owner without the existing registered owner being first notified and having the opportunity to object. This may avoid further human rights difficulties in land of registered title – but if the difficulty in *Beaulane Properties Ltd v Palmer* was that land might be lost through inadvertence, what about an owner who is notified of a squatter's application for registration but fails to realise the importance of the letter and so does not object in time?

Registration and fraud

Walter Green owned two farms in northern Lincolnshire, Gravel Hill Farm and Thoresway. Mr Green and his wife Evelyne had two sons, Geoffrey and Derek, and three daughters. In 1961 Mr Green decided to retire. He sold Thoresway to his younger son, Derek, for £75 per acre, which was well below the market price. The elder son, Geoffrey, was to have Gravel Hill Farm, but so as to avoid death duties Mr Green did not sell Gravel Hill Farm to Geoffrey, but instead granted him a right to demand to purchase it, at any time in the next 10 years, at a price of £75 per acre. The right to demand to purchase was a property right, known as an option. In the meantime, before he exercised the option, Geoffrey was given a lease of the farm.

The option should have been registered by the family solicitor in the Land Charges Register. If this had been done, it could have been asserted against anyone who bought the land from Mr Green. But, as Lord Denning, Master of the Rolls, said in the Court of Appeal:

strangely enough [the family solicitor] made a serious mistake. He ought to have registered the option ... under the Land Charges Act 1925. It was the simplest thing in the world to do. But he did not do it. Why he did not, no one knows. It is a mystery ... This mistake was afterwards to cost everyone dear ... For six years the family lived happily as families do ... Then something transpired which was to shake the family to its roots. Father Walter decided to deprive the elder son Geoffrey of the option. He met a lawyer somewhere or other and told him of the option. We do not know who this lawyer was. But he seems to have suggested to the father a way of getting out of the option. This lawyer said to father Walter: 'See if the option has been registered. If it has not been registered as a land charge, you can sell Gravel Hill Farm over the head of Geoffrey and get rid of the option.'

The option had not been registered. Mr Green told Evelyne and Derek.

Together the three of them hatched a plot ... It was that father Walter should sell Gravel Hill Farm to mother Evelyne for £500 and convey it to her. It was to be done quickly, without the elder son Geoffrey knowing anything about it. The conveyance was to take place before Geoffrey could exercise the option. Once the conveyance was executed, his option would be defeated ... Never in the history of conveyancing has anything been done so rapidly.

Derek Green's solicitor carried out the sale to Mrs Green, who paid £500 for the farm, which was worth between £40,000 and £50,000. But, '[a]s happens in families, one of them could not keep a secret. A rumour reached the elder son Geoffrey: "Father has sold your farm to mother for £500".'

Upon hearing of the sale, Geoffrey Green immediately sought to exercise the option, and his solicitors finally registered it on the Land Charges Register. 'But it was too late. Three weeks too late.' Geoffrey Green then began litigation, which was carried on after his death by his personal representatives, the Midland Bank Trust Company. Firstly he sued his father for damages for breach of contract: the option was a property right, but it was such a right because Walter Green had made a contract with his son of which the court would order specific performance, that is, the court would compel Walter Green to sell the farm to his son as agreed, and would not limit the son to money compensation. So it was open to Geoffrey Green to complain that there had been a breach of contract by his father in selling the farm to his mother. Secondly, Geoffrey Green sued his mother (and, after her death, her estate) claiming that despite the failure to register it, the option, as a property right, could still be asserted against his mother's estate, which could therefore be made to sell the farm to Geoffrey's estate for £75 per acre (by this time the land was worth up to £1,500 per acre on the open market). Thirdly, Geoffrey Green sued the family solicitors for damages for negligence in failing to register the option, and Walter Green (and subsequently his estate) for damages for conspiracy with Mrs Green to deprive him of the option.

The key element from the land law point of view was the question of whether the option could be asserted against Mrs Green's estate despite the lack of registration. In the High Court Mr Justice Oliver held that it could not be asserted. Geoffrey's estate appealed, and the majority in the Court of Appeal (Lord Denning and Lord Justice Eveleigh) held that it could (*Midland Bank Trust Co v Green* [1980] Ch 590). Lord Denning gave two reasons. First, the Land Charges Act 1925 only prevented the unregistered option being asserted against Mrs Green's estate if she had been a purchaser of the land 'for money or money's worth'. This, Lord Denning said, meant a 'fair and reasonable value', and since what had been paid was a 'gross undervalue', Mrs Green's estate could not rely upon the statute. Secondly, the registration requirement could not be used in order to commit a fraud, meaning 'any dishonest dealing done so as to deprive unwary innocents of their rightful dues'. The sale to Mrs Green had been made deliberately to deprive Geoffrey Green of his option, and since Mrs Green had been involved in the fraud, her estate could not take advantage of the non-registration. Eveleigh LJ agreed with Lord Denning as to the price. In his view the supposed 'sale' to Mrs Green was a sham; it was a gift, not really a sale at all, with £500 being paid as a token in an attempt to take advantage of the non-registration. (Eveleigh LJ did not refer to the possibility of an alternative approach based upon fraud.)

Both Lord Denning and Eveleigh LJ thus found that the option could still be asserted against Mrs Green's estate, despite the failure to register it. Sir Stanley Rees disagreed, taking a very different view of the facts. Lord Denning's emphasis had been upon a fraudulent 'plot'. Sir Stanley Rees, in contrast, pointed out that Mr Green had sold the farm to his wife after a serious illness, and that in her will Mrs Green had distributed shares in the farm so that each of the Green children would receive 20% of the value. Fraud indeed 'unravels all', and certainly there had been a scheme to defeat the option, but it appeared to have been entered into to redistribute the value of the family land among the children, and could not be regarded as a fraud. Moreover, although the £500 was very much below the true value of the land, it was nevertheless paid. The sale to Mrs Green was not a sham, and the £500 was 'money or money's worth' as the Land Charges Act 1925 required.

Mrs Green's estate then appealed to the House of Lords (*Midland Bank Trust Co v Green* [1981] AC 513). Lord Wilberforce, with whom the other four members of the court agreed, held that the option could not be asserted against Mrs Green's estate. The Land Charges Act 1925 was intended:

> to provide a simple and understandable system for the protection of title to land, [and] should not be read down or glossed; to do so would destroy the usefulness of the Act. Any temptation to remould the Act to meet the facts of the present case, on the supposition that it is a hard one and that justice requires it, is ... removed by the consideration that the Act itself provides a simple and effective protection for persons in Geoffrey's position, [that is] by registration.

In other words, the inability of Geoffrey's estate to assert the option against his mother's estate was Geoffrey's own fault: the Land Charges Act 1925 provided him with a simple means to protect his interest, and having failed to take advantage of it Geoffrey could not complain. In response to an argument that Mrs Green's estate could only rely on the lack of registration if she had bought the land in 'good faith', Lord Wilberforce pointed to the difficulty of disentangling the motives of the purchaser: '[s]uppose . . . the purchaser's motives were in part to take the farm from Geoffrey and in part to distribute it between Geoffrey and his brothers and sisters, but not at all to obtain any benefit for herself, is this acting in "good faith" or not?' And as to the argument that the £500 was not 'money or money's worth', even if £500 was nominal (which Lord Wilberforce doubted), it made no difference since 'money or money's worth' included a nominal sum. The House of Lords therefore reversed the decision of the Court of Appeal: the option could not be asserted against Mrs Green's estate.

Here is a key dilemma in land law. On the one hand registration rules aim for simplicity and clarity: registered property rights may be enforced against purchasers, most unregistered ones may not. Exceptions will not be made for those who fail to register. On the other hand, such clarity may seem to work injustice: those with rights in land who fail to realise that they should be registered may lose them if others take advantage of the registration rules. Where should the line be drawn? What is more important: certainty or justice – and are these ends entirely distinct anyway? And if there was no fraud in *Midland Bank Trust Co v Green* is it possible to think of similar situations in which fraud might be found?

Classifying interests: licences and leases

We have seen above that land law provides a series of pigeonholes into which property rights in land must be fitted. One of those pigeonholes is for leases. A lease involves a grant of exclusive possession of land, for a fixed or periodically renewable period of time, usually in return for payment of rent. The tenant under a lease has exclusive possession, and is thus able to exclude everyone, including the landlord, from the land. In contrast, a licence does not give exclusive possession. A lodger is a typical licensee, paying to live in someone's house without the right to exclude the owner from any part of the house.

Mr Agis Antoniades owed an attic flat in a house in Upper Norwood, London. He was approached in 1985 by Mr William Villiers who, with his girlfriend, Ms Sharon Bridger, had been looking for accommodation for three months. The attic flat comprised a bedroom, a bedsitting room, a kitchen and a bathroom. Mr Antoniades had a policy of not granting leases. He only granted licences. He did this to prevent occupiers of the flat being protected under the Rent Acts, which conferred rights against the landlord upon residential tenants under leases, but not upon licensees. He told Mr Villiers and Ms Bridger that he only dealt in licences. They each signed separate but identical documents, described as licences. Mr Antoniades was described as the licensor, and Mr Villiers and Ms Bridger were each described as a licensee. Each document provided, among other things, that the licensee agreed to pay £87 per month; that the licensee agreed to share the accommodation with the licensor, and with such other licensees as the licensor should from time to time permit to use the rooms; that the licensee would not permit anyone else to use the rooms; and that the 'real intention' of the parties was to 'create this licence which is not coming under the Rent Acts'. There was also a provision that if the licensee 'marrie[d] any occupier of the flat' he or she would give notice to vacate the flat. In other words, read literally, the agreements seemed to mean, as Lord Oliver put it in the House of Lords, that Mr Antoniades 'and an apparently limitless number of other persons' might move in 'to share the whole of the available accommodation, including the bedroom, with what, to all intents and purposes, was a married couple committed to paying £174 a month in advance'.

In 1986 Mr Antoniades gave Mr Villiers and Ms Bridger notice to leave the flat. They went to a rent officer, who decided that they were in fact tenants under a lease, not licensees, and so were protected from eviction under the Rent Acts. His Honour Judge Macnair in the Lambeth

County Court agreed, dismissing Mr Antoniades's action for possession of the flat. Mr Antoniades then appealed to the Court of Appeal, arguing that Mr Villiers and Ms Bridger were licensees (*Antoniades v Villiers* [1988] 3 WLR 139). The Court of Appeal agreed.

The leading case on the distinction between leases and licences, *Street v Mountford* [1985] AC 809, had been decided by the House of Lords in May 1985, a few months after Mr Villiers and Ms Bridger had moved into the flat. *Street v Mountford* was itself decided in the context of the application of the Rent Acts, and it was clear that the key question was whether the agreements had given Mr Villiers and Ms Bridger exclusive possession of the flat. It was also clear that the fact that the agreements were called licences did not necessarily mean that in law they were licences: as Lord Templeman had put it in *Street v Mountford*, 'Words alone do not suffice. Parties cannot turn a tenancy into licence merely by calling it one', and 'the court should ... be astute to detect and frustrate sham devices and artificial transactions whose only object is to disguise the grant of a tenancy and to evade the Rent Acts'.

It was clear that if the agreements with Mr Villiers and Ms Bridger were not a sham, they amounted to licences: under the terms Mr Villiers and Ms Bridger did not obtain the exclusive possession which was essential to a lease. But were the agreements a sham? Lord Justice Bingham thought not: 'If the written agreements are to be discarded as a sham, it must be shown not only that the occupants intended to enjoy a right to exclusive possession but also that the landlord shared that intention.' Since it was clear that Mr Antoniades did not intend to grant exclusive possession there was no sham. It would have been different if the clauses about sharing could not have been put into effect but, as the fact that Mr Villiers and Ms Bridger had had a guest to stay showed, the 'introduction of an additional sharer would not have been physically impracticable'. The other member of the court, Lord Justice Mann, agreed.

Mr Villiers and Ms Bridger appealed to the House of Lords, which overturned the Court of Appeal (*Antoniades v Villiers* [1990] 1 AC 417). Lord Templeman, who had given the leading judgment in *Street v Mountford*, held that the clauses permitting Mr Antoniades to share the flat with Mr Villiers and Ms Bridger, and to allow others to do so as well, were a pretence (Lord Templeman now preferred 'pretence' to 'sham'). Contrary to Bingham LJ's assessment, 'the facilities in the flat were not suitable for sharing between strangers', and had sharing genuinely been contemplated there would have been negotiations as to how it would work in practice. Moreover, Mr Antoniades had never in fact sought to share the flat, or to allow others to do so. The clauses about sharing were 'only designed to disguise the grant of a tenancy and to contract out of the Rent Acts'. The other members of the court agreed. As Lord Oliver put it:

> There is an air of total unreality about these documents read as separate and individual licences in the light of the circumstances that [Mr Villiers and Ms Bridger] were together seeking a flat as a quasi-matrimonial home . . . The unreality is enhanced by . . . the accompanying agreement not to get married, which can only have been designed to prevent a situation arising in which it would be quite impossible to argue that the 'licensees' were enjoying separate rights of occuption [and were not joint tenants under a lease].

It followed that the clauses about sharing could be ignored, in which case Mr Villiers and Ms Bridger did have joint exclusive possession, had taken a joint lease, not separate licences, and were therefore tenants entitled to Rent Act protection who could not be evicted.

Subsequent legislation has reduced the importance of the distinction between leases and licences in this context, but the decisions in *Street v Mountford* and *Antoniades v Villiers* make plain that land law's pigeonholes are in some cases mandatory. Despite agreement between the parties that what they have created is a licence, the legal conclusion that it is in substance a lease is inescapable. Agreements concerning land must be made against the background of the structure and policy of the law and its application by the judges. Land law indeed pervades our lives.

Reading list

FH Lawson and B Rudden, *The Law of Property*, (3rd edn, Oxford: Oxford University Press, 2002).

E Cooke, *Land Law* (Oxford: Oxford University Press, 2006).

6   Equity

Elaine Palser
Exeter College, Oxford

Equity is a subject of considerable practical importance in modern-day law. It is, however, also a subject that owes its existence (and principles) in large part to the historical deficiencies of other areas of law which it sought to address. It is therefore to this history that we must turn first in order to understand what equity is all about.

Historical development

During the Middle Ages the law, as administered by the Courts of Common Law, was very formalistic. In order to bring a successful claim, a claimant was required to fit the facts of his case within the rigid constraints of one of the set 'forms of action'. If he could not do that, then, whatever the merits of his case, he had no remedy in law. Furthermore, even if a claim were successful, the only remedy available was a monetary one (*damages*) – there was no way of preventing someone from doing something deemed to be unlawful or indeed of compelling him to do that which he ought to do.

Many people found themselves dissatisfied with the quality of justice being dispensed by these courts and therefore sought the assistance of the King, who was not constrained by the procedure or legal principles of the common law. Indeed, such was the demand for this royal justice that the King's Chancellor (whose responsibility it was to deal with these alleged cases of 'injustice') eventually established his own independent court, the Court of Chancery. The Court of Chancery's role was to mitigate the sometimes harsh effects of the formalistic laws and procedures of the Courts of Common Law and to ensure that a just outcome was achieved. In deciding in individual cases how best to exercise its discretion to ensure justice, the Court of Chancery over time began to develop its own rules, and these became known as the rules of equity. Although there are many different and varying rules of equity, as the word 'equity' suggests, their primary underlying objective is fairness and justice.

For many centuries the legal systems of common law and equity operated alongside each other, although increasingly the two systems were merged and that merger was completed by the Judicature Act 1873, under which the two systems were fused, so that today all courts must consider the rules of both the common law and equity.

Chancery's creations

The legacy of the Court of Chancery is an important and lasting one in today's legal system. Arguably, its most significant creation, and one we will look at in more detail below, is the *trust* (or *use* as it was originally known), by which a person may hold an interest in property separate from the formal legal ownership of the property.

The Court of Chancery was also responsible for the development of a range of different remedies, including: *injunctions*, by which a party is ordered to refrain from doing some particular act (a 'prohibitory injunction') or to perform some positive act (a 'mandatory injunction'); *specific performance*, which compels a defendant to perform his side of a contract; *rescission*, which allows a contract entered into on the basis of a misrepresentation to be terminated; and *rectification*, whereby mistakes in a written contract may be corrected. These remedies can be of considerable value to claimants in a variety of situations, particularly where damages alone simply would not be sufficient.

Injunctions are perhaps most notoriously used by celebrities to protect their privacy, whether by preventing the publication of potentially damaging photographs or stories or curtailing the invasive behaviour of the paparazzi. They are, however, also important in ordinary life. In a commercial context, for example, a company which is concerned that one of its debtors may try to hide or spend his money to avoid paying it may wish to obtain a 'freezing injunction' to prevent him from removing his assets from the country or otherwise disposing of them. In private life, an individual who has just ended a tempestuous relationship might seek an injunction preventing a violent ex-partner from coming within a certain distance of him or her.

The other remedies are also crucial in many contractual relationships, whether it be for a company seeking to avoid a multi-million pound contract entered into on a false basis (rescission) or a buyer seeking to compel a homeowner who has promised to sell his home to complete that purchase (specific performance).

All of the remedies available in the Court of Chancery were entirely at the court's discretion, and this discretionary element remains a feature of these equitable remedies. This means that the court has a power, but not an obligation, to award an equitable remedy, and in deciding whether to do so will weigh up a variety of factors according to the remedy sought. For example, where a party claims specific performance, the court will consider whether damages would be an adequate remedy. Damages will usually be appropriate in relation to a contract for sale of movable goods, such as a car; where, however, the object in question is land (which is always unique in character) or perhaps an important painting for which there can be no substitute, the court may well order specific performance as damages would not suffice.

Equitable maxims

In exercising their equitable powers, the courts often refer to one or more of the so-called 'maxims of equity', which, whilst not hard and fast rules, give general guidance on the way in which the court should exercise its jurisdiction.

One of the factors that a court will take into account when exercising its equitable jurisdiction is the conduct of the parties. This is embodied in two maxims: 'he who comes to equity must come with clean hands' and 'he who seeks equity must do equity'. The first is concerned with how the claimant has behaved in the past in relation to the matter in question. For example, a party seeking specific performance of an agreement for the transfer of land may be refused that equitable remedy if he has acted improperly in relation to that agreement (ie does not have 'clean hands'), such as by denying its existence in previous court proceedings. The second maxim looks to the intentions of the claimant – if he is not willing himself to behave fairly in relation to the matter in question, then he cannot rely on equity to his advantage. Thus, for example, a party to a contract will not be entitled to specific performance unless he is himself prepared to fulfil his side of the agreement.

A further, oft-cited maxim is that 'equity sees as done that which ought to be done'. This does not necessarily mean that a court will require a party to do what he should have done but that, when determining the parties' rights, it will assume that it was done. For example, where a person occupies a property on the basis of an agreement with the owner to enter into a lease on particular terms, but the lease has not been properly executed in accordance with the formal legal requirements for the creation of a valid lease, the parties may nevertheless be treated in equity as if the lease had been properly executed and thus be bound by its terms, such as the tenant's obligation to pay rent.

An introduction to trusts

We now move on to consider trusts, which constitute the main area of study in any Equity course. There is no definitive classification of trusts, but there are usually said to be three distinct types of trusts: express trusts, resulting trusts and constructive trusts.

Express trusts

Express trusts are deliberately and explicitly created by the parties, and recorded in much the same way as a contract. Let us consider an example. S, a wealthy grandfather, does not have long to live. He has one teenage grandson, B, aged 15, to whom he would like to leave £500,000. S is concerned, however, that B will squander all the money if he gives it to him now. He therefore transfers the money to B's father, T, and agrees with T that: the money is to be invested and the interest accumulated; T is to pay B £10,000 per annum until he reaches the age of 25; up to £100,000 may be withdrawn at any time for the cost of B's education; and when B reaches the age of 25 the remaining capital and interest are to be paid to him. What S has done is create an express trust. The creator of a trust is called the *settlor*. B is the one who will benefit from the trust so he is called the *beneficiary*. B's father, T, is the trustee, and he provides the link between the settlor and the beneficiary. T is said to have the *legal interest* or *legal title* whilst the beneficiary has a *beneficial interest*. T is under an obligation to invest and pay the money to B in accordance with S's wishes. In this way, S can ensure B is well provided for even after his death, and he avoids the risk of B squandering the money. This is an example of an *inter vivos trust*, which is a trust created by the settlor during his lifetime. Trusts may, however, also arise on a person's death in accordance with the terms of his will. These trusts are called *testamentary trusts* and the person making the will (and therefore making the testamentary trust) is called a *testator*. In the example given above, S could instead have chosen to provide for B in his will by way of a testamentary trust.

Express trusts are useful for a variety of reasons. They can, as in the example above, be used to provide income for family members whilst at the same time protecting the family assets in the longer term. They might also be used to provide income for incapacitated family members. For example, if parents have a disabled child who is unlikely ever to have a job, they might want to set up a trust fund for him so that they can be assured that he will have a steady income for his entire life, even after their death.

One of the principal uses of express trusts is in tax planning, where the capacity to split the legal ownership and beneficial interest in property can be used to redistribute assets in such a way as to reduce a person's liability to tax. For example, if your income exceeds a certain amount, your income above that threshold is taxed at a higher rate than income below it. Thus, a person liable to higher rate tax may transfer some of his investments to a trustee to hold them on trust for other members of his family who have a lower income and thus pay tax at a lower rate, thereby making a significant saving on his tax bill.

Trusts are also important in the context of charities. Charitable trusts are created to provide for one or more of the following specified purposes: the relief of financial hardship, old age, sickness or disability; the advancement of education; the advancement of religion; and other charitable purposes which help and benefit the community. For example, scholarships may be set up as charitable trusts for the purpose of education. Registered charitable trusts benefit from special treatment from the Government. In particular, they generally do not have to pay tax on their income and capital gains, and they can claim 'gift aid' on any donations made to them by a taxpayer, by which the Government increases the value of the donation by a fixed percentage.

Resulting trusts

Resulting trusts are not expressly created but arise by operation of law. There are two types of resulting trusts: *automatic resulting trusts* and *presumed resulting trusts*.

Automatic resulting trusts

An automatic resulting trust arises where an express trust fails either entirely or in part. For example, a settlor may transfer property to trustees on trust for X 'for life' (meaning X is to have the benefit of the property during his lifetime), but fail to say what is to happen to the property on X's death. On X's death, the trustees will hold the property on resulting trust for the settlor. The property is said to *result back* to the settlor. If the settlor has died, the property will result back to the settlor's estate and be distributed according to the settlor's will (or, if he has no will, according to the rules of intestacy, which determine how one's assets are to be distributed if one dies without a will). This type of resulting trust is called an automatic resulting trust simply because it arises automatically, by operation of law, without any action on the part of the settlor or trustees or anyone else.

Presumed resulting trusts

Presumed resulting trusts look to the settlor's presumed intention and are of two kinds: *purchase price presumed resulting trusts* and *gratuitous transfer presumed resulting trusts*.

Let us begin with purchase price presumed resulting trusts. Imagine X buys a house and the house is put into his name, but in fact X's friend, Y, paid the entire purchase price. X then holds the entire house on resulting trust for Y. This means that if the house is sold it is, in fact, Y who will be entitled to the entire sale proceeds. Similarly, if X is declared bankrupt, his creditors will not be able to obtain an order for the sale of the house to recover the debts because the house is held by X entirely for Y. Take the same scenario again, but this time let us assume that X and Y each paid half of the purchase price. X will then be holding the house on resulting trust for himself and Y in accordance with their respective contributions to the purchase price. This means that if the house is sold, X and Y will this time each get half of the sale proceeds.

A gratuitous transfer presumed resulting trust arises where Y owns a house and he transfers the house into X's name, without receiving any payment in return. X will then hold the property on resulting trust for Y because it is presumed that a gift was not intended.

In all these cases it is, however, possible to rebut the presumption of resulting trust by providing evidence to the contrary. For example, if Y contributed to the purchase price, X could produce evidence to show that it was a gift, or to clear a debt owed by Y to X. In the absence though of evidence to the contrary, the court will generally presume a resulting trust in these situations. Where, however, Y in the two examples given above is a man and X is his wife or child, there is a rebuttable presumption, called the presumption of advancement, that Y intended a gift, and accordingly no resulting trust arises. Rather archaically, this presumption does not apply if Y is the wife or mother.

Constructive trusts

Constructive trusts also arise by operation of law in a variety of circumstances, generally where the courts have found that it would be inequitable for the legal owner of property to have full beneficial ownership. It is, however, difficult to discern any overarching characteristic which unifies all constructive trusts and it is therefore best to look at those situations where the case law has found a constructive trust to have arisen. For example, where a company director abuses his position in order to obtain money for himself (whether by taking a bribe, misappropriating funds or using confidential information to his advantage), the money may be held on a constructive trust because he acquired it in breach of his fiduciary duty to the company. Another common area in which constructive trusts arise is the family home, considered in detail later on.

Some examples

Creating an express trust

In order to create an express trust, three things need to be clear: first, that the settlor intended to create a trust (*certainty of intention*); secondly, what property is subject to the trust (*certainty of subject matter*); and thirdly, what, or whom, the trust is for (*certainty of objects*). These requirements are referred to as the *three certainties*.

Certainty of intention

In establishing certainty of intention, it is necessary to look at the precise wording of the provision. Phrases such as 'on trust to' and 'to my trustees' are usually indicative of an intention to create a trust. The wording should also be mandatory, and precatory words, such as 'in the hope', 'in the belief' or 'in confidence', will generally not suffice. In the example, '£100,000 to my trustees to distribute as they see fit amongst my grandchildren', there is certainty of intention: the words 'to my trustees' are indicative of the intention to create a trust and the phrase 'to distribute' is mandatory. In contrast, '£100,000 to Diana, hoping that she will distribute the money amongst my grandchildren' contains the precatory phrase 'hoping that' and so will probably be treated simply as an outright gift to Diana of £100,000, leaving Diana with nothing more than a moral obligation (not a legally enforceable one) to distribute the money amongst the grandchildren. However, the court will look at all the circumstances in assessing whether there was an intention to create a trust. If, instead of leaving the money to Diana, the testator had, using the same words, left it to his bank or his solicitor or 'to my trustees', the court may well take the view that it is unlikely the money was intended to be an outright gift (as those are not parties one would usually intend to benefit) and would give effect to the testator's wish that it be distributed amongst his grandchildren, despite the use of precatory words.

Certainty of subject matter

In the example given above – '£100,000 to my trustees to distribute as they see fit amongst my grandchildren' – the subject matter is £100,000 and that is certain. Equally, if the provision specified some tangible asset, such as a car or a house, provided that the asset was sufficiently identified, there would be certainty. If, of course, a settlor owned two houses and had simply said 'my house', there would not be certainty of subject matter. Tangible assets can pose particular difficulties if they are to be split between two or more beneficiaries. Take the following provision of a will: 'My collection of fine porcelain dolls to my trustees who must distribute half to Christina and half to Charlotte.' It is clear that the subject matter is the testator's fine collection of porcelain dolls. However, the provision requires half to be distributed to Christina and half to Charlotte, with no indication as to which dolls should go to which beneficiary. It will therefore fail for uncertainty of subject matter and Christina and Charlotte will not receive the porcelain dolls. Where one is dealing with tangibles (whether they be porcelain dolls, cases of fine wines, or jewellery) that are to be split, or to only part of which the trust applies, it is necessary to segregate the items because each tangible item is identifiable and different. Even where the items may be very similar, such as bottles of wine in the same case, it has been held that, for example, one bottle may be corked while another is not, and therefore a trust that does not segregate them must fail for uncertainty. However, in the case of intangible assets (such as money, shares and other investments) identification of the particular assets is unnecessary because such assets are always going to be indistinguishable from one another, and the value of the assets can simply be divided as provided in the trust without any prior segregation.

Certainty of objects

In most cases, the third requirement – certainty of objects – is satisfied by the existence of defined beneficiaries. In the example – '£100,000 to my trustees to distribute as they see fit amongst my grandchildren' – the beneficiaries are the testator's grandchildren. Assuming he does in fact have grandchildren, the certainty of objects requirement is met. In most cases, there is clarity with regard to the beneficiaries, but this is not always the case. Consider: '£100,000 to my trustees to distribute as they see fit amongst my clever former pupils'. The class of beneficiaries, whilst defined, is conceptually uncertain: what is meant by 'clever'? Does it mean everyone who has got an A in each subject each year, anyone who has ever got an A, anyone who has averaged an A overall throughout her school years, or none of these options? It is impossible to tell. Indeed, even if it just referred to 'my former pupils' that too might be uncertain as it is not clear whether a pupil whom the testator had taught just for a few days would qualify. Again, it is not possible to be certain who is entitled to benefit. Such conceptual uncertainty can render a trust void.

Another type of uncertainty is evidential uncertainty, which arises where the class of beneficiaries is conceptually capable of definition, but on the facts it is not possible to be certain of the actual beneficiaries. If, for example, the testator in our example had worked at a large number of schools over a considerable period, it may be impossible to draw up a complete list of her former pupils, should a complete list be required.

A means of getting around the problem of conceptual and evidential uncertainty may be to delegate it (although there is some debate as to whether conceptual, as opposed to evidential, uncertainty can be delegated). For example, if the testator had worked at one school all her life, she could provide that the headmistress of that school is to determine who qualifies as 'clever', or she may expressly leave it up to her trustees to determine.

In considering issues of certainty, a distinction should also be drawn between a fixed trust and a discretionary trust. With a fixed trust, the trustees have no discretion whatsoever as to which beneficiaries should benefit from the money or the respective shares they should receive. An example would be: '£100,000 to my trustees to distribute in equal shares amongst all my grandchildren'. Thus, if there are say four grandchildren, the trustees must distribute £25,000 to each of them. As such, it is essential that the trustees can draw up a complete list of all the beneficiaries so that they can distribute the money in accordance with the trust. The trustees of a discretionary trust, on the other hand, have some discretion as to who is to benefit and/or the share each beneficiary is to receive. For example: '£100,000 to my trustees to distribute equally amongst such of my grandchildren as my trustees see fit' or '£100,000 to my trustees to distribute in such shares as they see fit amongst all my grandchildren'. Here the trustees have a discretion as to which grandchildren (in the first example) and the size of their shares (in the second example). With a discretionary trust of this sort, it is not necessary to draw up a complete list of all possible beneficiaries. The test which applies here is the so-called 'given postulant' test. This means that the trust will be valid even if a complete list cannot be drawn up, provided that it is possible to say with certainty whether any given individual is or is not a member of the class of beneficiaries. Where this test applies, it is thought that only conceptual, not evidential, certainty is required.

In addition to conceptual and evidential uncertainty, there is a third strand to the requirement of certainty of objects: that the class of beneficiaries is not administratively unworkable. This is typically the case where there is a defined class of beneficiaries, but it is simply too large to be administered sensibly. For example, a trust for the benefit of all the inhabitants of Oxfordshire, even if it were sufficiently conceptually certain (which is questionable), would probably fail for administrative unworkability. This overlaps to some extent with the fourth potential ground for uncertainty, which is described by the courts as 'capriciousness'. Capriciousness extends beyond mere breadth of numbers and applies where the terms of the trust negate any sensible intention on the part of the settlor, such as perhaps a trust for the benefit of all redheads in Oxfordshire.

So far, we have considered the certainty of the objects where those objects are the beneficiaries of the trust. The object of a trust might, however, be a purpose rather than a person. Purpose trusts (other than charitable trusts) are generally void because there is no beneficiary able to enforce them, although there are a handful of (not particularly logical) exceptions, including trusts for the maintenance of a particular animal and trusts for the erection and maintenance of monuments or graves. So, if Dennis wished to ensure that his cat, Tiddles, was properly provided for after his death, whilst he cannot make Tiddles (not being human) a beneficiary, he might create a purpose trust: '£10,000 to my trustees for the purpose of ensuring that my beloved cat, Tiddles, is looked after for the remainder of her life'.

Where a trust fails for lack of certainty of subject matter or objects, the assets will 'result back' to the settlor (or, in the case of a testamentary trust, the testator's estate) on a resulting trust. In the case of a testamentary trust, the assets will then be distributed either according to the provisions (if any) in the testator's will relating to the distribution of the residue of the estate or, if that fails, according to the law of intestate succession. Where, however, there is found to be no certainty of intention, the assets may instead be treated as an outright gift to the purported trustee, as in the case of Diana given above.

Constructive trusts of the family home

Where two people (X and Y) live together, but the legal title to their home is in X's sole name, the court may conclude that Y is nevertheless entitled to a beneficial interest in the property and impose a constructive trust. This means that X, as the legal owner, holds the property on trust with the beneficial interest in the property split (not necessarily equally) between X and Y. It can do this regardless of the relationship between the parties: X and Y could be husband and wife, civil partners under the Civil Partnership Act 2004, unmarried heterosexual cohabitees, unregistered homosexual cohabitees, elderly parent and adult child, or just friends.

Often the legal niceties of the ownership of the family home are of little concern. There are, however, a number of situations in which the question of ownership becomes crucial. For example, if X is declared bankrupt or does not keep up repayments on his mortgage, his creditors will only be entitled to seize that part of the property to which he is beneficially entitled, and that part which he holds on constructive trust for Y will thus be protected. Equally, when a relationship breaks down, if Y has invested a lot of money and/or effort in the home over a number of years, she might well wish to establish an interest in it. This is of particular importance in cases where the relationship is not a marriage or civil partnership and thus the court's statutory powers to redistribute the assets (in a divorce or dissolution of a civil partnership) are not applicable, although it is still useful to identify the interests of all the parties in the event of divorce or dissolution.

If X and Y draw up in writing an express trust as to their respective shares in the home, provided that they comply with the necessary formalities and the three certainties considered above, this will be conclusive and there is no need to venture into the realm of constructive trusts. It is, however, quite rare for family members to have gone to such lengths, and constructive trusts therefore often prove very important.

In what circumstances will a constructive trust of the family home arise? The current leading case in this area is *Lloyds Bank plc v Rosset* [1991] 1 AC 107. In this case, Mr and Mrs Rosset bought (in Mr Rosset's sole name) a semi-derelict property with a view to renovating it. Mrs Rosset supervised the renovation work and did a lot of the decoration herself, but she made no direct contribution to the purchase price. Subsequently the marriage broke down, Mr Rosset defaulted on a loan which was secured on the property, which the bank then sought to repossess, and Mrs Rosset accordingly claimed (unsuccessfully) a beneficial interest in the property. Lord Bridge (at pp. 132–133) set out the principles to apply in determining whether a constructive trust should be imposed:

> The first and fundamental question which must always be resolved is whether, independently of any inference to be drawn from the conduct of the parties in the course of sharing the house as their home and managing their joint affairs, there has at any time prior to acquisition, or exceptionally at some later date, been any agreement, arrangement or understanding reached between them that the property is to be shared beneficially. The finding of an agreement or arrangement to share in this sense can only, I think, be based on evidence of express discussions between the partners, however imperfectly remembered and however imprecise their terms may have been. Once a finding to this effect is made it will only be necessary for the partner asserting a claim to a beneficial interest against the partner entitled to the legal estate to show that he or she has acted to his or her detriment or significantly altered his or her position in reliance on the agreement in order to give rise to a constructive trust or proprietary estoppel.

> In sharp contrast with this situation is the very different one where there is no evidence to support a finding of an agreement or arrangement to share, however reasonable it might have been for the parties to reach such an arrangement if they had applied their minds to the question, and where the court must rely entirely on the conduct of the parties both as the basis from which to infer a common intention to share the property beneficially and as the conduct relied on to give rise to a constructive trust. In this situation direct contributions to the purchase price by the partner who is not the legal owner, whether initially or by payment of mortgage instalments, will readily justify the inference necessary to the creation of a constructive trust. But, as I read the authorities, it is at least extremely doubtful whether anything less will do.

Thus, for a constructive trust to arise: (a) there must have been a common intention (express or inferred) to share the beneficial interest in the property; and (b) the claimant must have relied on that common intention to her detriment. Let's look at these two elements.

Common intention

Where there is direct evidence of an express agreement between the parties to share the property, then it is not necessary to look any further into the conduct of the parties in order to establish a common intention.

Conversely, where no such explicit agreement is found, the common intention must be inferred from the conduct of the parties. In this regard, only direct financial contributions to the purchase price (whether initially or by way of mortgage instalments) will justify the inference of a common intention. Other contributions – such as paying household bills, doing the cleaning, cooking and washing, caring for the children and decorating the house – are all irrelevant to inferring common intention in the light of *Rosset*. Thus, if Y pays all the household expenses and X pays the mortgage, Y will not have a share, but if they happened to reverse those roles, Y could acquire a share.

This restrictive approach is a marked retreat from the position in the pre-*Rosset* case of *Eves v Eves* [1975] 1 WLR 1338 in which a man bought a house as a joint home but put it into his sole name, telling his partner (falsely) that she was too young to be able legally to own property. The claimant made no financial contribution to the purchase price but did a great deal of work renovating the home and caring for her partner and the children. When they separated, she claimed a share of the house. The Court of Appeal imposed a constructive trust under which she was entitled to a quarter share in the house, Lord Denning focusing on the fact it would be inequitable in the circumstances to deny her a share. In the absence of an express agreement or direct contributions to the purchase price, Mrs Eves' claim would have failed under the new approach in *Rosset*.

Detriment

Common intention alone is, however, not sufficient to establish a constructive trust. The claimant must also show that she acted to her detriment; that is, she expended money and/or effort for which she was not otherwise rewarded. If there is direct evidence of an express agreement, arrangement or understanding (an express common intention) that the property is to be shared beneficially, then any relevant act by the claimant to her detriment, whether envisaged by the agreement or not, will give rise to a constructive trust. Where a common intention has been inferred on the basis of direct financial contributions, these contributions will serve to establish detriment.

In *Grant v Edwards* [1986] Ch 638, CA, Browne-Wilkinson VC said: 'setting up house together, having a baby and making payments to general housekeeping expenses … may all be referable to the mutual love and affection of the parties and not specifically referable to the claimant's belief that she has an interest in the house', but 'once it has been shown that there was a common intention that the claimant should have an interest in the house, any act done by her to her detriment relating to the joint lives of the parties is … sufficient detriment to qualify. The acts do not have to be inherently referable to the house'. In the same case, Nourse LJ said that the conduct required 'must be conduct on which the woman could not reasonably have been expected to embark unless she was to have an interest in the home'.

Share size

The final question that must be answered by the court, if it finds that a constructive trust arises, is the size of the claimant's entitlement.

In *Oxley v Hiscock* [2004] 3 All ER 703, now the leading case on this issue, Mrs Oxley and her partner, Mr Hiscock, purchased a property in Mr Hiscock's sole name. A constructive trust was found to arise on the basis that both parties had contributed (albeit unequally) to the purchase price. There was, however, no evidence of any discussion between them as to their respective shares. When the house was sold, Mrs Oxley sought a declaration from the court that she was entitled to half of the proceeds of sale. Chadwick LJ stated (at p. 737) that in some cases the answer to the question of the appropriate share size will be determined by evidence of what the parties said and did at the time of the acquisition. In the absence of such evidence:

> ... the answer is that each is entitled to that share which the court considers fair having regard to the whole course of dealing between them in relation to the property. And, in that context, 'the whole course of dealing between them in relation to the property' includes the arrangements which they make from time to time in order to meet the outgoings (for example, mortgage contributions, council tax and utilities, repairs, insurance and housekeeping) which have to be met if they are to live in the property as their home.

This approach gives the courts a considerable degree of discretion to determine what they consider to be a fair share in the circumstances. As such, whilst it might be a rare victory for 'fairness' (for those who passed the more restrictive hurdle of establishing a common intention), it is likely to make predicting the outcome with any degree of accuracy extremely difficult. In *Oxley*, it was held that, given that there had been a pooling of resources and conduct consistent with an intention to share the outgoings referable to ownership and cohabitation, it was fair that Mrs Oxley should receive a greater share than that she would have been entitled to based on her direct contribution alone. However, it would be unfair to Mr Hiscock, who had contributed substantially more to the purchase price than Mrs Oxley, for the property to be split equally. Accordingly, a fair division of the proceeds of sale was 60% to Mr Hiscock and 40% to Mrs Oxley.

Criticisms

The approach taken by the courts to the imposition of constructive trusts of the family home, which has fluctuated somewhat over the past 40 years, may be subject to a number of criticisms.

The first – and perhaps socially most significant – criticism is the apparently discriminatory effect of this approach against women, who are more often the ones who stay home and look after the house and children and make substantial non-financial contributions. In the absence of an express common intention, they will lose out unless they make some (however trivial) direct contribution to the purchase price. This result arguably runs contrary to the explicit recognition by the courts of the importance of such indirect and even non-financial contributions when determining a fair share.

The second criticism is that this approach does not give proper effect to the common intention of the parties. On the one hand, by making direct financial contributions a strict prerequisite of inferring common intention, the courts run the risk of disregarding other, often substantial, evidence of the parties' intentions. On the other hand, by imposing a constructive trust whenever direct financial contributions are made, there may be no critical consideration of whether that really does evidence any common intention.

A third, and related, criticism is that the finding of a common intention can be artificial. In *Grant v Edwards* [1986] Ch 638, for example, the court held that there was a common intention even though Mr Edwards, in whose sole name the property was brought, had falsely told Mrs Grant, his partner, that the property could not be put into their joint names because it would cause complications with her divorce. It is difficult to see how there could have been a genuine intention on Mr Edwards's part to share the property.

Fourthly, it may be argued that the reliance, when inferring common intention, on direct financial contributions has blurred the distinction with resulting trusts. As we noted above, resulting trusts arise whenever a party has contributed towards the purchase price of a property. However, the parties' respective shares under a resulting trust are directly proportionate to their contributions to the purchase price, whereas in the case of a constructive trust it is clear that other, broader issues will be taken into account in determining fair shares.

Of course, many of these criticisms belie the fact that these constructive trusts may not, in truth, be about common intention. In Canada, the courts emphasise that the defendant would be unjustly enriched if the claimant were to receive no share in the property, and in New Zealand, the courts focus on the reasonable expectations (rather than the shared intentions) of the party claiming an interest in the property. Back in England, however, this area of law remains uncomfortably torn between giving effect to the true intentions of the parties and seeking to achieve a 'fair' result in all cases.

Reading list

S Gardner, *An Introduction to the Law of Trusts* (2nd edn, Oxford: Oxford University Press, 2003).

DJ Hayton, *The Law of Trusts* (4th edn, London: Sweet & Maxwell, 2003).

AJ Oakley, *Parker and Mellows: The Modern Law of Trusts* (8th edn, London: Sweet & Maxwell, 2003).

JE Penner, *The Law of Trusts* (4th edn, Oxford: Oxford University Press, 2004).

PH Pettit, *Equity and the Law of Trusts*, (10th edn, Oxford: Oxford University Press, 2006).

7 Contract Law

Nicholas J McBride
Pembroke College, Cambridge

Introduction

Someone enters into a contract if he makes a binding – legally enforceable – promise to someone else. So the 'law of contract' tells us in what situations someone will make a binding promise to someone else, and what remedies will be available if that promise is breached. While academics refer to the area of law dealt with in this chapter as 'contract law' or the 'law of contract', it is more helpful to think of it as 'contracts law' or the 'law of contracts'. This is because there are at least three different ways of making a binding promise to someone else, and therefore at least three different *types* of contracts recognised in English law. They are as follows.

Covenant

Someone enters into a covenant if he makes a promise in a deed. (A deed is a particular kind of legal document. It has to be signed and witnessed to be valid.) Promises made in deeds will automatically be binding, other things being equal. The requirements that have to be satisfied in order to make a deed are laid out in the Law of Property (Miscellaneous Provisions) Act 1989. A document will only amount to a deed if it makes it clear on its face that it is intended to be a deed; if it has been signed by the person making the deed or his representative, and the signature has been witnessed; and the deed has been 'delivered' (which simply means that the person making the deed has made clear his intention to be bound by it).

Bilateral contract

A bilateral contract arises if two people enter into an agreement under which they each promise to do something for the other. Under the contract, each party is bound to do what they promised to do for the other under their agreement. For example, if you and I agree that I will mow your lawn next Saturday, and that you will pay me £50 for doing so, we will have entered into a bilateral contract – my promise to mow your lawn next Saturday will be binding on me, and your promise to pay me £50 if I do so will be binding on you. The contract is bilateral in nature because each of us is bound to do something for the other under it.

Unilateral contract

A unilateral contract arises if I make a promise to you with the object of inducing you to act in a particular way. If you do so act, my promise to you will be binding on me. For example, suppose I promise to pay you £100 if you find and return to me my lost dog, Freddy. You immediately start searching for Freddy. As soon as you start searching for Freddy, my promise to pay you £100 if you find and return Freddy will be binding on me. I made that promise with the object of inducing you to search for Freddy, and my promise had the effect of inducing you to search for Freddy. So if you do find Freddy and return him to me, I will have to pay you £100. The contract that arises in this situation is unilateral in nature because only one person is bound to do something under it: me. You don't have to search for Freddy if you don't want to. But if you do search for Freddy, then I will have to pay you £100 if you find him and give him back to me.

Estoppel

There is no reason to suppose that the number of types of contracts recognised in English law will always be fixed at three. In other words, there is no reason to suppose that there will only ever be three ways of making a binding promise to someone else under English law.

For example, American and Australian law has recognised the existence of what might be called the *estoppel contract*. This type of contract arises where A makes a promise to B and B relies on that promise in such a way that it would be unfair to allow A to break his promise. (This contract is called an *estoppel* contract because A is said to be 'estopped' from going back on his word.)

For example, suppose that Egghead University is in negotiations to buy a precious manuscript for £1m. Dives has agreed to fund the acquisition, but just before the negotiations are completed, there is a dramatic fall in the stock market and Dives loses a lot of his wealth. As a result, Dives tells Egghead that he can't help fund the purchase. Egghead asks an old member, Croesus, to help out. Croesus reluctantly tells Egghead that he will stump up the £1m needed if no one else can be found to pay for the manuscript. No one else is willing to help fund the purchase of the manuscript, but Egghead goes ahead and contracts to buy the manuscript for £1m, thinking that Croesus will fund the purchase. Croesus then tells Egghead that he has changed his mind – he won't be contributing a penny towards the cost of purchasing the manuscript.

Is Croesus's promise to pay Egghead £1m binding on him? Under English law, it would seem not. The promise was not made in a deed. Croesus's promise to pay Egghead £1m did not form part of a bilateral contract. His promise was not made as part of an agreement under which Croesus and Egghead undertook to do things for each other. And Croesus's promise to pay Egghead £1m does not seem to have given rise to a unilateral contract either. Although Egghead relied on Croesus's promise by contracting to buy the manuscript, Croesus did not make his promise with the object of inducing Egghead to buy the manuscript. Almost certainly, Croesus would have been overjoyed if the negotiations to buy the manuscript had fallen through: he would then have been released from his promise to pay Egghead £1m.

So Croesus's promise to pay Egghead £1m will not be binding on him under English law. In contrast, the American and Australian courts would probably recognise that Croesus's promise was binding on him under an estoppel contract. The fact that Egghead foreseeably, reasonably and irretrievably relied on Croesus's promise makes it unfair for Croesus to go back on his word, and as a result he would be bound by his promise to give Egghead £1m. It should be noted that the concept of an estoppel contract is not unknown in English law. If A promises not to enforce a debt owing to him by B, and B relies on that promise in circumstances where it would be unfair for A to go back on his word and enforce the debt, then an estoppel contract will arise, and A will be bound by his promise not to enforce the debt. Again, if A promises to grant B an interest in land belonging to A, and B relies on that promise in circumstances where it would be unfair for A to go back on his word and refuse to grant B that interest, an estoppel contract will arise and A will be required to give B the interest that he promised to give him. However, the English courts have yet to take the step of building on these developments and recognising the existence of estoppel contracts in cases such as Croesus's case, where there was no promise to waive a debt or grant someone else an interest in land.

Should the English courts take this step? Should the mere fact that a promise has been relied upon in circumstances that make it unfair for the promisor to break his promise suffice to make the promise binding under English law? Obviously, if it would be unfair for the promisor to break his promise then there is a case for the State to intervene and force the promisor to keep his promise. Moreover, as we have seen, English law recognises that *some* promises – such as promises to grant someone else an interest in land, or promises to waive a debt – *can* give rise to estoppel contracts. Given this, it is hard to see why English law does not say that *any* kind of promise will be binding if it has been relied upon in circumstances that would make it unfair to break it. On the other hand, recognising the existence of estoppel contracts in cases such as Croesus's case would make the law on when a promise will be binding extremely uncertain. How can we tell with any certainty when the courts would find that it would be 'unfair' for someone to break a promise that has been relied upon? On balance, it seems that the unfairness involved in allowing people like Croesus to break their promises is a price worth paying to avoid this uncertainty. The fact that promises such as Croesus's could be made binding by the simple device of inserting them in a deed means that genuine cases of unfairness created by the English courts' current refusal to recognise the existence of estoppel contracts in cases such as Croesus's will be few and far between.

A double-edged sword

There are, of course, immense benefits in having a system of contract law. Without it, it would be very difficult to rely on the promises of anyone but one's friends and family and therefore very difficult to plan for the future. This is particularly important in the marketplace. It would be impossible for two businesses to make any long-term deals and give effect to them if they were not legally binding.

Suppose, for example, that Egghead University projects that it will need 2,500 computers a year for the next 10 years. Magic Computer plc makes computers of the type needed by Egghead University. In return for getting guaranteed sales of 2,500 computers a year for 10 years, Magic Computer would be willing to sell their computers to Egghead for a special discount price of £300 a computer. There is a deal to be struck here which would benefit both parties – but if it were not legally binding, it would be impossible to make the deal and then put it into effect. Distrust would prevent the parties coming together. Magic Computer would think, 'We can't commit ourselves to supply Egghead with 2,500 computers a year. We'd have to take on a lot more workers, and buy a lot more parts, to manufacture the computers – and then after we manufactured the computers, Egghead could make a nonsense of our investment and hard work by refusing to pay for them and buying computers from our rivals.' Egghead would think, 'We can't commit ourselves to buying 2,500 computers a year from Magic Computer. Admittedly, they're currently available at a bargain price – but after we'd bought the first batch and designed all our systems around them, what would stop Magic Computer from jacking up the price of the next batch of computers?' Fortunately, the projected deal between Magic Computer and Egghead would be binding – it amounts to a bilateral contract. And it is precisely the bindingness of the deal that allows Magic Computer and Egghead to enter into it and plan their affairs around it – to the benefit of both parties. (It should be clear from the foregoing that the reason why the law enforces bilateral contracts is because doing so allows parties in the marketplace to make and implement long-term deals with each other.)

There is, then, no denying the value of the English law of contract – indeed, modern life would be unimaginable without it. However, the existence of the law of contract does give rise to a range of potential problems. Chief among these is the problem of people trying to use the law of contract to *take advantage* of other people. For example, suppose that Sandy is driving to Greenville, where she has an important appointment. In order to get to Greenville, she has to go across Blue Lake in a ferry. The only available ferry is run by Red Ferry plc. Normally, when travelling on a ferry, Sandy would have a right under the Occupiers' Liability Act 1957 that the ferry company take reasonable steps to see that the condition of the ferry is such that she will be reasonably safe while travelling on the ferry. Before she is allowed to go onto the ferry, Sandy is presented with a form which says, among other things: 'I hereby waive any rights I might have that Red Ferry take care for my safety while on the ferry.' Sandy is told that unless she signs the form she will not be allowed on the ferry. She has no real choice but to sign. Sandy subsequently breaks her leg slipping on a concealed patch of oil on the deck of the ferry. Sandy sues Red Ferry for compensation. In its defence, Red Ferry argues that Sandy is bound by her promise to waive any rights she might otherwise have had that Red Ferry take reasonable steps to ensure that she was reasonably safe on the ferry.

Here Red Ferry is trying to use the law of contract to escape its legal responsibilities to Sandy. What is the best way for the law to deal with this kind of advantage-taking? Four responses suggest themselves.

Do nothing

This response is not actually as stupid as it sounds. The idea is to leave it up to the *free market* to eliminate Red Ferry's advantage-taking. If enough customers become dissatisfied with the way they are being treated by Red Ferry, then another ferry company will see an opportunity to compete with the service that Red Ferry provides across Blue Lake. The rival company will start running ferries across Blue Lake, advertising itself as a 'kinder, gentler' company than Red Ferry – one which takes care of its customers and isn't afraid to pay compensation when it gets things wrong. At that point, Red Ferry will be faced with the choice of either smartening up its act, or losing all its customers and going bust. Either way, Red Ferry's advantage-taking will not last.

However, this response to Red Ferry's advantage-taking suffers from a couple of problems. First of all, it involves the law tolerating Red Ferry's advantage-taking for as long as it lasts, with the result that any claims made against Red Ferry by injured customers such as Sandy will be dismissed on the ground that their promises to waive their rights are binding on them. Secondly, it is too optimistic to think that Red Ferry's treatment of its customers will allow a competitor to put it out of business. It may be that the money Red Ferry saves by treating its customers so harshly allows it to offer very cheap deals to cross Blue Lake that could not be matched by a 'kinder, gentler' company – and it may well be that faced with the choice, the general public would prefer to get a cheap fare from Red Ferry and take the chance of not being able to sue if they get injured than pay more to cross Blue Lake, safe in the knowledge that they will be protected if they are injured due to the fault of their ferry company.

Review

This response involves examining the promise made by Sandy and declaring it not to be binding if it was 'unfair' or 'unreasonable'. This response to wrongdoing is embodied by the Unfair Terms in Consumer Contracts Regulations 1999, which provide that 'An unfair term in a contract concluded with a consumer by a [business] seller or supplier shall not be binding on the consumer' (reg 8(1)) and further provide that 'A contractual term which has not been individually negotiated shall be regarded as unfair if, contrary to the requirement of good faith, it causes a significant imbalance in the parties' rights and obligations arising under the contract, to the detriment of the consumer' (reg 5(1)). So if it is judged that holding Sandy to her promise to waive her rights against Red Ferry would be 'unfair', given all the circumstances, then it will not be binding on her and Red Ferry will not be entitled to take advantage of it to escape their responsibilities to Sandy.

The problem with this response to advantage-taking is that it leaves people like Sandy in a state of uncertainty as to what their rights are. Suppose Sandy was consulting a solicitor about whether she could sue Red Ferry. The solicitor tells Sandy, 'You *would* have an excellent case – but the problem is that form you signed, waiving your rights against Red Ferry. If that's binding on you, then your case is doomed to fail.' Sandy asks, 'Well – is it binding on me or not?' The solicitor replies, 'Well, that depends on whether it would be "unfair" to hold that it is binding on you. If it would be "unfair", then it's not binding, and you'll win your case. If it wouldn't be "unfair" to hold you to your undertaking to waive your rights, then it will be binding on you, and you'll lose.' Losing her patience slightly, Sandy asks, 'Well – would it be "unfair" or not?' Sighing, the solicitor replies, 'Well, that's hard to tell. The courts' general approach will be to ask: did the form, contrary to the requirement of good faith, cause a significant imbalance in the rights and obligations between Sandy and Red Ferry to Sandy's detriment? And in order to answer that question, they'll look at all the circumstances of the case.'

It is immediately obvious that Sandy will have a big incentive not to carry on with her case against Red Ferry. She simply won't have enough confidence that she will win the case to enable her to take the chance of carrying on with it, losing and having to cover Red Ferry's legal costs (which are likely to be substantial). So whether or not the form in Sandy's case was actually binding on her or not will be irrelevant. The mere existence of the form – and the law saying that the form may, in certain circumstances, be binding on Sandy – will be enough to discourage Sandy from continuing with her claim against Red Ferry. So this second form of response to Red Ferry's advantage-taking – saying that Sandy's waiver of rights will not be binding on her if it would be 'unfair' to hold her to it – sounds eminently reasonable in theory. However, in practice it provides Sandy with an utterly useless form of protection against Red Ferry's advantage-taking.

Automatic strike-out

This is a very powerful response to Red Ferry's advantage-taking. Under it, Sandy's waiver of her rights against Red Ferry is automatically declared not to be binding on her. This response to Red Ferry's advantage-taking is embodied by s 2(1) of the Unfair Contract Terms Act 1977, which provides that, 'A person cannot by reference to any contract term or to a notice … exclude or restrict his liability for death or personal injury resulting from negligence.' (Section 1(3) of the same Act makes it clear that it only applies to attempts to exclude or restrict 'business liability'.)

Unlike the previous response to Red Ferry's advantage-taking, this response does not leave people like Sandy in a state of uncertainty as to what their rights are. Replay the above conversation between Sandy and her solicitor, this time factoring in the existence of s 2(1) of the Unfair Contract Terms Act 1977. This time round, the solicitor starts the conversation by telling Sandy, 'You have an excellent case against Red Ferry – that form you signed waiving your rights against Red Ferry is no problem: it's simply not binding under s 2(1) of the Unfair Contract Terms Act 1977.' End of conversation.

Despite its virtues, there is one problem with this response to Red Ferry's advantage-taking. Suppose that Red Ferry was forced into making all its customers sign the form that Sandy signed because it had been swamped by a large number of claims for compensation by people who had slipped on the decks of Red Ferry's ferries while crossing Blue Lake. (Ferries are, after all, very slippery places.) Almost all of these claims had no merit (in Red Ferry's view), but they were almost always for such small amounts that no individual claim was worth the expense of fighting. But added together, the claims amounted to a substantial expense that Red Ferry could not afford to incur. So they came up with the idea of getting all their customers to sign a form, waiving their rights that Red Ferry take care to see that they were reasonably safe while crossing Blue Lake. So whenever a claim for compensation was made against Red Ferry by a customer who had slipped on their ferry, the claim would be very easy and cheap to fight. Red Ferry could simply produce the customer's form and his case would be dismissed on the ground that the customer's waiver of rights was binding on him.

Section 2(1) of the 1977 Act prevents Red Ferry solving its problem with unmeritorious litigation in this way. Their forms will not work to protect them from being sued. As there seems no other way round Red Ferry's problem, s 2(1) of the 1977 Act might eventually work to drive Red Ferry into insolvency, sunk by a tidal wave of groundless claims which it has been made powerless to resist by s 2(1). So s 2(1) may in the long run work to the detriment of all the customers who need Red Ferry's services to cross Blue Lake.

Prior restraint

The fourth response to Red Ferry's advantage-taking is to allow the government to order Red Ferry to stop making its customers waive their rights against Red Ferry if Red Ferry's doing so is 'unfair' or 'unreasonable'. This response to advantage-taking can be found in the Unfair Terms in Consumer Contracts Regulations 1999, which empower the Director General of Fair Trading to order a business to remove a term from its contracts if he or she judges it to be 'unfair' under the Regulations. (If the Director General makes a mistake in applying the Regulations, the affected business can apply to the courts and ask them to set aside the Director General's order.)

This is a superior response to advantage-taking than any we have yet considered. If Red Ferry is acting unfairly or unreasonably in requiring its customers to waive their rights, then it will be made to stop, and any customer who is injured while on one of Red Ferry's ferries will not be in any uncertainty as to what his or her rights are because he or she will never have been made to waive them in the first place. At the same time, Red Ferry retains the liberty to require its customers to waive their rights when it would be 'fair' or 'reasonable' to do so – which it may well be if Red Ferry is forced into taking such a step in order to avoid being swamped with groundless claims for compensation that threaten to tip the company into insolvency.

However, there are grounds for concern about this response to advantage-taking. It involves granting the government unprecedented powers to meddle in the running of businesses, dictating the terms on which they will be allowed to trade. This cure may well turn out to produce effects far worse than the disease it was intended to treat.

The bindingness of contracts

It is a common error to think that a promise has to be written down to be legally binding. Perhaps Sam Goldwyn, the film producer, made this mistake when he joked that, 'A verbal contract isn't worth the paper it's written on'. In fact, very few promises have to be made in writing in order to be legally binding. The most notable example is a promise to convey land to someone else. This must be put down in writing (Law of Property (Miscellaneous Provisions) Act 1989) and inserted in a deed (Law of Property Act 1925, s 52(1)) to be binding.

But Goldwyn was not wholly wrong. There *are* cases where a promise that is supposedly binding under English law will not be worth the paper, if any, it is written on. Suppose, for example, that Liam agreed to buy a particular car on Paula's second-hand car lot for £5,000. A couple of problems with the car needed attending to: Paula promised that she would have those fixed and that she would then deliver the car to Liam's house. Liam promised Paula that he would give her the money for the car when she delivered it. Paula then rang Liam up a few days later to tell him she was going to sell the car to someone else, who had offered £6,000 for it. What remedies will Liam be entitled to in this situation?

Could he get the courts to order Paula to hand over the car to him, through the award of what is called an order of *specific performance*? This is unlikely. If the courts judge that getting Paula to pay Liam damages will adequately compensate him for the losses suffered by him as a result of Paula's breach of contract, then they will not make an order for specific performance against Paula. If the car in question is unique or of great sentimental value, thus making it hard to put a financial value on the loss that Liam will suffer as a result of not getting the car, then damages might not be an adequate remedy and then an order of specific performance might well be available. But let's assume the car in question is an ordinary, run-of-the-mill car and there is as result no question of Liam being awarded an order of specific performance in this case.

So Liam can't get specific performance, but he can sue for damages to compensate him for the losses suffered by him as a result of Paula's breach. So how much will he be able to sue Paula for? Well, let's assume that Liam can buy a virtually identical second-hand car for £4,500 to replace the one that Paula has failed to deliver to him. Can we say that Liam has lost £4,500 as a result of Paula's breach? No, we can't. We're overlooking the fact that Liam agreed to pay £5,000 for the car Paula was going to deliver him, and that Paula's breach means that he no longer has to pay her that sum. So Liam has actually saved £500 as a result of Paula's breach (the difference between the £5,000 that Liam would have had to lay out had Paula performed, and the £4,500 that Liam is now going to have to shell out to buy a car to replace the one that Paula failed to deliver to him). So Liam has suffered no loss as a result of Paula's breach. Does that mean that Liam cannot sue Paula for anything by way of damages in this situation? Not quite. The courts will award Liam *nominal damages* of £5 as acknowledgement that he has been the victim of a breach of contract.

So in this situation Paula has committed an obvious and deliberate breach of contract and all she has to pay Liam as a result is £5. It is hard to avoid the impression that Paula's binding promise to deliver the second-hand car to Liam wasn't worth the paper, if any, it was written on. Some would see this as a good result. Liam hasn't suffered any loss as a result of Paula's conduct, so why should he be able to sue her? Indeed, from one point of view, it would be positively regrettable if the law did anything to encourage Paula to keep her promise to Liam. The second buyer – the one who offered Paula £6,000 for the car – obviously valued the car much more than Liam, who was only willing to pay £5,000 for it. If you take the view that resources should go to those who value them most – where you are counted as valuing a resource more than anyone else if you are ready and willing to pay more for it than anyone else – then you will take the view that it was a good thing that Paula broke her promise to Liam and gave the car to the second buyer.

Others are more disturbed at the prospect of someone being allowed to flout their legal obligations without any kind of effective sanction. (In any case, the view that resources should go to those who are ready and willing to pay the most for them is extremely questionable. If you had a bowl of rice and had a choice between giving it to a starving child who had no money to pay for it, and a rich man who was willing to pay a pound for it because he had been suddenly seized with a desire for some Chinese food, it simply cannot be true that you should give the bowl of rice to the rich man and not the starving child.) Some effective sanction would be provided for Paula's breach if Liam were allowed to sue her for what might be called *restitutionary damages* – that is, damages designed to strip Paula of some or all of the gains she made by breaching her contract with Liam. This would allow Liam to sue Paula for some or all of the £1,000 profit that she made by selling the second-hand car to the second buyer, as opposed to Liam. The courts have recently started allowing claims for restitutionary damages to be made in breach of contract cases. However, they have made it clear that such damages will not be available in cases such as Liam's, where someone has contracted to buy goods from a seller, and then the seller has sold to someone else because he has received a better offer. (Evidently the courts also believe this sort of behaviour is to be applauded and not discouraged.)

A very effective sanction for Paula's breach would be provided if Liam were allowed to sue her for *punitive damages* (otherwise known as *exemplary damages*) – that is, damages designed to punish Paula for cynically and deliberately breaking her contract with Liam. However, while punitive damages may be awarded against people who commit torts, the courts have always set their face against such damages being awarded against people who commit breaches of contract. It is hard to see why this is so: some breaches of contract (such as an unjustified failure to pay up on an insurance contract protecting one in the event of ill health or unemployment or losing one's house) can be far more devastating than some torts for which punitive damages may be awarded. However, there is no prospect of the current position being reversed.

Reading list

J Adams and R Brownsword, *Understanding Contract Law* (4th edn, London: Sweet & Maxwell, 2000).

P Atiyah and S Smith, *Atiyah's Introduction to the Law of Contract* (6th edn, Oxford: Clarendon Law Series, 2006).

H Collins, *The Law of Contract* (4th edn London: LexisNexis UK, 2003).

E McKendrick, *Contract Law: Text, Cases and Materials* (2nd edn, Oxford: Oxford University Press, 2005).

8 Family Law

Jonathan Herring
Exeter College, Oxford

Family law is about chaos. In some areas of the law people will consult a lawyer before they act. Generally people do not create trusts, sign wills or set up companies without first consulting a lawyer. This means that the law can effectively regulate the way trusts, wills or companies are created. Unfortunately (or perhaps not!) people do not consult lawyers before having sex, moving in with someone, or even getting married. Indeed family lawyers are often only approached after a relationship has broken down. Family law is left to try and impose some order and justice on the messiness of people's lives that results from the ending of an intimate relationship.

Family law at most universities is an optional subject, but it is a very popular one. Popular because it is about the things that really matter: not money or profit, but love, relationships and families. The facts of the cases are easily understood, although the solution is often far from straightforward. And this reflects an important point. In many areas of family law the courts are left with a wide discretion: to decide what order will promote the welfare of the child, or what financial order on divorce will be fair. This discretion is necessary to enable the court to reach the decision which is correct for the particular individuals in the particular set of circumstances before it. After all everyone is different and everyone's family is different so it is not possible to develop hard and fast rules that apply to everyone's intimate relationships. That said, it should not be thought that the results in family law cases are utterly unpredictable. There are general principles which tend to govern many cases but they are normally in the form of presumptions, which can be rebutted if the circumstances indicate otherwise. For example, there is a presumption that on divorce or separation a child should keep in contact with both parents. However, if, say, the father has been a violent man, the court may decide that the presumption is rebutted and that it is not in the best interests of the child to retain contact with him.

There is, therefore, a tension in family law between having a broad discretion so that each case can be decided 'on its own facts' and providing some guidelines so that it is not up to the whim of each judge how she decides a particular case. Couples who are in dispute often do not want to have to go to court to resolve their disagreements and prefer to negotiate a settlement. But it is difficult to do so if no one has any idea how the court will deal with a particular case.

A major challenge to the discretionary basis of family law has been the Human Rights Act 1998. Some of the issues which were previously based on an assessment of what was fair, reasonable or would best promote the welfare of a child can now be argued in terms of rights. Later on in this chapter we will consider the issue of whether a father who is no longer living with his children has a right to see them (a right to have contact). Traditionally family law has approached such questions by asking, will it promote the child's welfare to have contact with her father? With the Human Rights Act in mind some lawyers believe the question should start with the principle that a child has a right to see her father. Or that a father has a right to see his child. These rights can be overridden if the exercise of the right would cause the child serious harm. The use of rights in this way has given the law greater predictability.

A major theme in family law is the issue of fault. In the past the family law courts were very keen on making moral judgments and declaring one party to be at fault. Hence a woman who committed adultery could be regarded as 'immoral' and therefore unfit to have a child living with her (the same rule did not seem to apply with such ferocity to men!). Similarly on divorce the courts were keen to declare whose conduct had caused the breakdown of the relationship. Indeed before 1970 one had to prove that adultery or cruelty had taken place in order to get a divorce. This meant that sitting in the back of the divorce courts would be a fascinating day out. Hotel chambermaids would be called in to give evidence about what they saw when they went to deliver breakfast in bed to room number 24. Nowadays, divorce hearings are far less intriguing. The courts are much more wary about declaring who is at fault. There is no longer any need to prove fault in order to get a divorce. You can either rely on the say-so of the parties (if they agree that one party has committed adultery or behaved in an unreasonable way) or a couple can obtain a divorce after living apart for two years without proving fault.

More generally in family law the courts have become unwilling to declare one party to be blameworthy in their conduct. A case much more representative of the current approach of the courts to fault is *Re W (Minors) (Residence Order)* [1999] 1 FLR 869 where a mother and father had separated. The mother and her new boyfriend took up naturism. The father sought a court order preventing the mother and her boyfriend being nude in front of the children. The Court of Appeal said this was an issue on which the court could not express a definite view. Within society there were a number of different views over the benefits and disadvantages of naturism and the court should not interfere. This reflects an apparently increasing reluctance in the courts to declare certain forms of conduct immoral. That said, in relation to domestic violence the courts are (at last) taking a stricter line. At one time that was regarded as a private matter, but now it is regarded as a matter which the courts will treat seriously.

Children are at the heart of many issues in family law, and the principle is that the court should make decisions which best promote the welfare of the child. Indeed this principle is found in s 1 of the Children Act 1989, the most important statute on the law relating to children. It means that when the court is resolving a dispute over what should happen it is the best interests of children which should be key. What is most convenient for the parents or, even, what may seem fairest from an adult point of view is not taken into account. So in *M v M* [1999] 2 FLR 737 where a father who had been in a motorcycle accident and suffered brain injuries sought to have parental responsibility for his child he lost. The court found that he did not have the mental ability to make decisions about the child. This was harsh on him because it was accepted that he loved the child, but the court was only concerned with what was in the child's best interests.

This principle, although a key one in family law, is not without its difficulties. The first thing to note is that the principle does not apply to all issues relating to family law. For example, a child cannot prevent her parents divorcing on the basis that the divorce will harm her, nor could a child ask the court to order her parents to give her all their money on the basis that that would promote her welfare! Secondly, it should be noted that the idea of looking only at the interests of the child, but not the parents, is problematic. Consider this scenario (one that has troubled the courts on several occasions): a child's parents have separated and the child is now living with her mother, but seeing her father regularly, which she enjoys. The mother's parents have become aged and need the mother's help. She wants to move to another part of the country so she can be close to them and take up a new job she has been offered. If she moves the child will see less of the father. You might think that, just considering this from the child's point of view, the court could make an order preventing the mother from moving. However, it is not that straightforward. If the mother cannot move and has to take regular lengthy journeys to see the parents and she is not able to take up the new job, this might cause the mother emotional and psychological harm. And if the mother is suffering this might affect the children. The issues in this kind of case are brought even more sharply into relief when the mother wishes to move to another country. The point is, though, that just considering the interests of the child on their own is difficult. The child's interests are often intertwined with the parent. What will harm the parent will harm the child, and vice versa.

Let us now consider in more detail three issues which have concerned family lawyers.

The rights of teenagers

Imagine these two scenarios:

(a) Kate, aged 14, wishes to have cosmetic surgery on her nose. Her parents strongly oppose this. Should the law permit her to have the surgery without her parent's consent?

(b) Dave, aged 14, does not want to have cosmetic surgery. His parents think he should. Should the law permit his parents to arrange a 'nose job' without his consent?

It may be surprising to learn that the answer to both these questions appears to be 'yes'. How did the law reach that rather strange position?

The leading case on children's rights is *Gillick v Norfolk and Wisbech AHA* [1986] AC 112. Mrs Victoria Gillick was the mother of four daughters. She was concerned about guidance issued by the Department of Health which indicated that it would be appropriate for a GP to give contraceptive advice or treatment to a child under the age of 16 even without parental consent. Mrs Gillick sought a court order that the guidance was unlawful. She argued that if a doctor wished to provide non-urgent treatment to one of her daughters under the age of 16 then her consent was required.

In the House of Lords Mrs Gillick lost. But only just: two judges agreed with her, three did not. The majority held that if a child is sufficiently competent to understand the issues involved she can give a legally effective consent to receive treatment. Where the child was competent there was no need for parental consent to be obtained, or even for the parent to be notified. Indeed if the doctor did tell the parent what the child had said this would be an unlawful breach of confidentiality. However, their lordships did agree that normally a doctor should encourage a child to discuss sensitive issues with her parents. Their lordships also emphasised that doctors could only provide treatment to a child which they thought was in the best interests of the child.

The decision of the House of Lords in *Gillick* generated much excitement among family lawyers. It appeared that for the first time their lordships had acknowledged that there was not an unbreachable gulf between adults and children, which hitherto had meant that adults could make decisions as to how to live their lives, but children had no rights to decide how to live their lives. Some commentators thought the era of children's rights had arrived.

But, the case law was to take a surprising turn. In *Re W* [1993] Fam 64 the Court of Appeal had to deal with a girl who was suffering from anorexia nervosa and was refusing treatment for her condition. The Court of Appeal found her not to be competent, but considered the legal position were she to be competent. The Court of Appeal held that the House of Lords in *Gillick* had held that a competent child could give effective consent to treatment, but that did not mean that if she was competent her parents were *not* able to give consent on her behalf. The Court of Appeal explained that if a doctor were to treat a child this could amount to a criminal offence or a tort unless the doctor had a defence or legal 'flak jacket', as they called it. This could be provided by either the competent child (as the House of Lords in *Gillick* had made clear) or by a parent with parental responsibility for the child or by a court order.

The effect of the Court of Appeal's interpretation of *Gillick* was that a child has the right to say 'yes' (a right to consent to treatment) but not a right to say 'no' (because a parent can give consent and override the child's refusal). To many academics this is an illogical position for the law to take. If a child is competent to make a decision the law should respect that decision whether the child consents or not. Indeed, if a child is to have a right to be able to consent or refuse medical treatment the law should respect the right to say 'no' more than the right to say 'yes'. To return to the example given earlier: if Kate's desire to have cosmetic surgery is not met, this will, no doubt, be frustrating to her, but she only has to wait until she is 18 and then she can consent. However, if Harry's desire not to have surgery done is not met this is a far graver infringement of his rights. It is far worse to have surgery imposed upon you that you do not want than to be refused surgery that you do wish.

But, it is submitted that the law is not illogical. The mistake was to see *Gillick* as a case about children's rights (although it did appear to be that at the time). It should instead be seen as a case about preventing parents from vetoing treatment which doctors regard as being in the best interests of children. The key point in *Gillick* was that their lordships wanted doctors to be able to give children the medical treatment they need. The law is now set up to be as easy as possible for doctors to be able to do this: they can if they have the consent of either a competent child, or a person with parental responsibility or, if necessary, the courts. So perhaps *Gillick* was not a case about giving children the right to receive the medical treatment they wanted, but rather a case about ensuring that children receive the medical treatment they need.

Disputes over frozen embryos

One of the features of family law is that changes in science and culture are constantly throwing up new dilemmas for the law to deal with. Issues which were unproblematic just a few decades ago, with no questions worth thinking about, can now become the subject of books. So, not long ago the question of who was a child's father was relatively unproblematic. But in the age of sperm donation and with the number of children raised by step-parents the question is far from straightforward for courts in the UK and Europe.

One issue troubling the courts in the UK was that concerning a dispute over a frozen embryo. The facts of the case (*Evans v Amicus Healthcare Ltd* [2004] 3 All ER 1025) were this. In October 2001 Natalie Evans and Howard Johnston, who were engaged, underwent IVF treatment. It was discovered that Natalie Evans had tumours on her ovaries. Her ovaries had to be removed as soon as possible and she was required to make a decision quickly on whether she wanted any ova removed and frozen. There were three main options: either that she freeze her ova; or her eggs be fertilised with donated sperm and frozen; or that her ova were fertilised with Mr Johnston's sperm and then frozen. She chose the last option, a decision she would subsequently deeply regret. There were two main reasons for it. The first was that frozen ova do not freeze well and many do not survive. The second was that Mr Johnston assured her that he wanted to be the father of her children; that they were not going to split up; and that she 'should not be negative'. Six eggs were harvested, fertilised and frozen. Later that month her ovaries were removed. In May 2002 the couple separated and Mr Johnston wrote to the clinic asking for the embryos to be destroyed. Ms Evans sought an order preventing the destruction of the embryos. This is a case on which people hold deeply divided views. Some believe strongly that if Mr Johnston wanted the embryos destroyed he should be allowed to have them destroyed. Others believe that Ms Evans should have been allowed to use the embryos.

The Court of Appeal found the case straightforward in legal terms and decided against Ms Evans and authorised the destruction of the embryos. The Human Fertilisation and Embryology Act 1990 (HFEA 1990) makes it clear that a licensed infertility clinic is only permitted to store an embryo if there is an effective consent by each party whose gametes have been used to bring about the creation of the embryo (HFEA 1990, Sch 3, paras 6(3) and 8(2)). If at any time either provider of the gametes withdrew their consent to the storage, the embryo had to be destroyed. As a matter of interpretation of the HFEA 1990 there was little dispute over the correct application of the case.

The Court of Appeal also thought that the decision was correct as a matter of principle. It would be wrong for a child to be born to a father who did not want the child to be born. That would be contrary to a child's welfare. Secondly the court regarded it as an important principle underlying the HFEA 1990 that a person who provided eggs or sperm to a clinic could control what happened to their eggs or sperm. You might not be convinced by these points. After all many children are born in circumstances in which their fathers do not want them to be born. In any event, is it right to say that it would be better for the child not to be born at all than to be born to a father who did not want it? In a case of natural sexual intercourse leading to a pregnancy there is nothing the man can do about it if the woman wants to go ahead and give birth. It may be that these points indicate that asking what is in the welfare of the child yet to be born is rather problematic. Indeed except, perhaps, in a case where a child would be born with appalling disabilities, it might be difficult to imagine circumstances in which it would be better for the child not to be born. As to the second argument that people should control their gametes, in this case it was not possible to permit both Ms Evans and Mr Johnston to decide what should happen to their gametes once they had been mixed. Their views were in conflict and it was necessary to decide whose view should carry greater weight.

Here the issue of human rights can be brought into play and human rights were discussed by the Court of Appeal. In simple terms Ms Evans was claiming the right to be a parent. She wanted to use the embryos to become pregnant and to raise the child. As we have already said, in normal sexual intercourse once the man has released his sperm he cannot stop the woman going ahead and giving birth to any child so conceived. Why should Ms Evans be treated differently because she is suffering from infertility and needs to use medical assistance? On the other hand Mr Johnson was seeking to rely on the right not to be a father. What a grave infringement of a man's rights it would be if his sperm could be taken and used to produce a child against his wishes. He did not want the burdens and responsibilities of parenthood, especially with a woman with whom he was no longer in a relationship. The Court of Appeal thought that both of the claimed rights – the right to be a parent and the right not to be a parent – could fall within Art 8 of the European Convention on Human Rights which protects the right to respect for private and family life. The court decided that in effect the two rights were equal and it was not possible to protect both parties' rights and therefore the destruction of the embryos was justifiable under the European Convention.

Not everyone agrees with the Court of Appeal's assessment that the rights were equal. You could go back to what is at the heart of the rights claimed here. In essence this is the right of autonomy: the right to live your life as you wish. It is common to talk in terms of people having the right to find and live out their version of the 'good life' free from interference from the State. This provides us with some benchmark against which to measure these competing rights. Would it be a greater setback to their version of living their 'good life' for Ms Evans to be denied having the child she so desperately wanted, or for Mr Johnston to have to live his life knowing there was a child of his whom he did not want?

When the case went to the European Court of Human Rights (*Evans v UK*, Application No 6339/05) the question was whether the approach taken in England through the HFEA 1990 was incompatible with the European Convention on Human Rights. The European Court of Human Rights held:

> The Court accepts that a different balance might have been struck by Parliament, by, for instance, making the consent of the male donor irrevocable or by drawing the 'bright-line' at the point of creation of the embryo. It notes in this regard that this latter solution has been adopted in a number of Member States of the Council of Europe ... However, the central question in terms of Article 8 of the Convention is not whether a

different solution might have been found by the legislature which would arguably have struck a fairer balance, but whether, in striking the balance at the point at which it did, Parliament exceeded the margin of appreciation afforded to it under that Article. In determining this question, the Court attaches some importance to the fact that, while, as noted above, there is no international consensus as to the point at which consent to the use of genetic material may be withdrawn, the United Kingdom is by no means alone among the Member States in granting to both parties to IVF treatment the right to withdraw consent to the use or storage of their genetic material at any stage up to the moment of implantation of the resulting embryo. *(para 68)*

In other words the European Convention on Human Rights would have permitted a country to have a law making the man's consent to the use of his sperm irrevocable from the moment he had provided it.

Two judges (Judges Traja and Mijovi) in the European Court of Human Rights dissented. They thought that the approach taken by the HFEA 1990 was too rigid, given that it was denying such an important right of Ms Evans:

> The real question, however, is whether in striking such a rigid balance the legislature was right to give the party withdrawing consent a totally controlling position and to accord that party's Article 8 right a presumptive value. We think that the exceptional situation of the applicant, who has no other means of having a genetically-related child, should have been made a matter of a deeper consideration by the domestic authorities, and that they were under an obligation to secure her right to become a mother in her exceptional circumstances. Denying the implantation of the embryos amounts in this case not to a mere restriction, but to a total destruction of her right to have her own child. In such a case the Convention case-law is clear and does not allow a State to impair the very essence of such an important right, either through an interference or by non-compliance with its positive obligations. We do not think that a legislative scheme which negates the very core of the applicant's right is acceptable under the Convention. *(para 2)*

You might be wondering whether there was not a claim that the embryos had interests that the law should protect. The Court of Appeal explained that under English law embryos have no rights or interests of their own. Not everyone would agree with this summary of the law in England, but this is not the place to go into that. The European Court of Human Rights explained that the embryo could not claim a right to life under Art 2. It was explained that the legal position of the embryo was a controversial issue among those countries who had signed the European Convention on Human Rights. It was within each State's 'margin of appreciation'. In other words each country which had signed the Convention could decide its approach for itself. This meant that if an individual country wanted to protect the embryo within its law it could, but also a country could decide that the embryo would not be so protected.

Contact between parents and children

A few years ago a man dressed as Batman got onto the roof of Buckingham Palace, while another man threw purple powder at the Prime Minister in the House of Commons. This was the work of a group entitled Fathers 4 Justice. It (and other groups) have complained that the family courts have treated fathers unfairly. A particular source of complaint is over the courts' treatment of 'contact cases'. Where a couple separate they (or the courts) must decide with whom the child should live and how often the child should see the other party. Sometimes couples agree (or the courts order) *joint residence*: that the child spend an equal amount of time with each parent. However, often the parents live a long distance apart or the 'work commitments' of the parties mean that joint residence is not possible. Where the couple cannot agree the matter needs to go to court.

Despite the impression you might get from the press the courts are very keen to make contact orders. In 2004 the courts made 70,169 contact orders and refused to make a contact order in 504 cases. Claims therefore that the courts are 'anti-fathers' in refusing to make contact orders are unfounded. Indeed the number of cases where contact orders are not made looks surprisingly low given that the cases which tend to go to court are the most controversial where there are allegations that the father has been abusive to the mother or children. However, Fathers 4 Justice and similar groups do have a point about the enforceability of contact orders.

The problem is this. The court may make an order that the mother allows the father to see the child, say, every other weekend. However, the mother may simply refuse to allow the father to see the child. What is the court to do then? One option is to imprison the mother. That is, after all, what we do normally when someone refuses to comply with a court order. However, this is problematic. Imprisoning the mother is only likely to harm the child. The whole point about family law is meant to be promoting the welfare of the child and that is the principle justifying making the contact order in the first place. It looks a bit odd to make an order in order to promote the welfare of the child and then enforce it in a way which harms the child. Worse than that, the order may be counterproductive. If a child sees her father applying to court for the imprisonment of her mother, that may turn the child against the father and mean it is even less likely than it might have been that the child will have effective contact with the father. So what about transferring residence to the father? Well, the courts have done that in a few cases. But often the father is not in a position to undertake primary care of the child: his work commitments may not enable that. The court may also not be convinced that it is appropriate for him to be the child's primary caretaker. If so, the court may feel it can do nothing.

But doing nothing leaves the courts looking stupid. They have made an order which they cannot then enforce. Some fathers' groups have indeed complained that contact orders are not worth the paper they are written on because the courts are reluctant to enforce them.

What this shows is the weakness of law. Lawyers like to think that the law is all mighty. All problems can be solved by law's magic powers. They cannot. The problems over contact cases demonstrate this. If anything can resolve these complex cases it is negotiation, mediation and counselling rather than legal proceedings. Even those are, in my view, unlikely to be effective. Research suggests that by far the most common reason mothers have for not allowing fathers contact to the children is that they fear that they themselves will be subject to violence at the hands of the father or their children will be. Indeed the number of children and partners killed in the course of contact disputes indicates that these fears may not be utterly far-fetched. Nevertheless these are fears which the courts have decided are unfounded in such cases and have ordered contact. However, just because the courts say that the fears are ungrounded does not mean that mothers accept that. Hence it is that threats of prison are rarely effective. What parent would not go to prison rather than subject her child to the perceived risk of violence?

We have not yet mentioned rights. Much of the discussion of this issue in recent years has centred on the concept of rights. It is said that fathers have a right of contact with their children, or more commonly that children have the right of contact with their fathers. If children have a fundamental right of contact with their fathers, should not the courts enforce those rights by imprisonment of mothers, even if that does harm the child?

This argument is interesting. It overlooks the following point. If children do have a fundamental human right of contact with their fathers, the courts should not only enforce this against mothers who are seeking to restrict contact between a child and a father, but also against fathers who simply do not want to see their children. In fact far more children do not see their fathers because the fathers do not want to have contact, than because the mother is preventing contact. The danger in this debate is that the phrase 'a child's right to contact' is taken seriously when the father wants to have contact with the child, but is ignored when he does not. This is often a danger with children's rights claims. As children's rights can often not be enforced by the children themselves, there is a danger that they are picked up and enforced only when to do so is in the interests of a particular adult. Note this is not, as such, an argument against children's rights, but a reason why we must be very careful that children's rights do not become a tool with which to pursue adult agendas.

Conclusion

Family lawyers live in interesting times. Looking to the future there are some interesting issues. Will the impact of human rights thinking mean that greater emphasis is placed on the rights of individuals and less emphasis on the obligations that flow from parenthood or marriage? Undoubtedly in the past family law has worked against the interests of women, but some feel now that it is men that are disadvantaged by it. But is the 'male backlash' justified given the continued rates of domestic violence and child abuse largely perpetrated by men? Will we see an increase in acceptance of children's rights or will worries over child abuse and children's anti-social behaviour lead to an increasingly protective or coercive attitude towards children? Time will tell. One thing is for sure: family law is not going to stop being any less fascinating.

Reading list

S Cretney and R Probert, *Cretney's Family Law* (London: Sweet & Maxwell, 2003).

G Douglas, *An Introduction to Family Law* (2nd edn, Oxford: Oxford University Press, 2004).

J Herring, *Family Law* (2nd edn, Pearson Education, 2004).

9   EU Law

Dr Andrej Savin
Emmanuel College, Cambridge

Understanding the EU

Students approaching European Union law for the first time often have difficulties understanding how it works and what it does. It may seem to them to be more in the domain of international conventions than law, poorly understood but fervently enforced from Brussels, an ever increasing menace to national sovereignty. In addition to that, whereas it may intuitively be clear what criminal, contract or tort laws do, it is not so with EU law. Indeed, what laymen often think of as falling under EU law, such as the Schengen visa regime, may not, strictly speaking, form the mainstream of EU regulation or may not even be subject to it.

The aim of this brief introduction is to give a very basic idea of the main goals of the European Union, its institutions, its main principles and one of its main legislative areas – the Single Market.

What does the EU do?

The aims that the European Union pursues are described in Art 2 of the EC Treaty:

> Article 2
>
> The Community shall have as its task, by establishing a common market and an economic and monetary union and by implementing common policies or activities referred to in Articles 3 and 4, to promote throughout the Community a harmonious, balanced and sustainable development of economic activities, a high level of employment and of social protection, equality between men and women, sustainable and non-inflationary growth, a high degree of competitiveness and convergence of economic performance, a high level of protection and improvement of the quality of the environment, the raising of the standard of living and quality of life, and economic and social cohesion and solidarity among Member States.

These tasks are primarily economic: a common market and an economic and monetary union is created and the Union has as its tasks the promotion of notably economic aims, such as non-inflationary growth. This does not mean that the Union pursues no other aims. Indeed, it must be clear that at least the pursuit of 'social cohesion and solidarity' involves non-economic devices. Furthermore, in achieving the economic aims, it is often necessary to regulate in non-economic fields. So, a further list of EU activities can be found in Art 3 of the EC Treaty, and these include:

(a) an internal market characterised by the abolition, as between Member States, of obstacles to the free movement of goods, persons, services and capital;

(b) a system ensuring that competition in the internal market is not distorted;

(c) a policy in the sphere of the environment;

(d) a contribution to the attainment of a high level of health protection;

(e) the association of the overseas countries and territories in order to increase trade and promote jointly economic and social development;

(f) a contribution to the strengthening of consumer protection.

Article 3 states that, in all the activities referred therein, 'the Community shall aim to eliminate inequalities, and to promote equality, between men and women'.

How did the EU develop?

Historically, the European Union is one of many of Europe's incarnations, not the first and likely not to be the last. The first economic union after World War II was the European Coal and Steel Community (ECSC) in 1951, followed by the European Economic Community (EEC) and Euratom in 1957. The institutions of the three were merged in 1965, and the EEC changed its name to the European Community (EC) in 1987. The Treaty of Maastricht of 1992 created the European Union, comprising the European Community in what was called the 'first pillar' of EU constitutional structure, and adding two more 'pillars': one dealing with Common Foreign and Security Policy (CFSP), the other with Justice and Home Affairs (JHA). The pillars shared the institutions but the defining constitutional principles, some of which will be discussed below, operated only in the first. This effectively rendered the European Community the most effective of the three.

At present, the Union faces many challenges, not least of which is the latest wave of enlargement, brining the total number of Member States to 25. The new members bring a much-needed work force and increase the total population by about one-third. Economically, however, they are currently below the EU average, adding only about 3 to 4% to the Gross Domestic Product. Leaving cultural differences aside, the EU faces the dilemma of effectively regulating a Union with such a large number of members and citizens.

How does the EU regulate?
What laws exist in the EU?

The main sources of EU law are: Treaties, regulations, directives, decisions and judgments of the European Court of Justice.

At present, several *Treaties* coexist as sources of EU law and a number of historical ones have been incorporated into the original EC Treaty. The first document, the European Coal and Steel Treaty from 1952, has been superseded by more recent ones. The original Treaty is the Rome Treaty (commonly referred to as the 'EC Treaty'), entering into force in 1958, and afterwards revised on a number of occasions, including by the Single European Act in 1987, the Maastricht Treaty in 1993, the Amsterdam Treaty in 1999 and the Nice Treaty in 2003. The most important recent attempted change is the failed Draft Treaty establishing a Constitution for Europe.

Regulations have the force of law the moment they are published in the *Official Journal*. This feature is called *direct applicability*. In fact, not only are Member States not required to implement a regulation but they are also forbidden from doing it. They are powerful instruments, sometimes indicating the extent to which national sovereignty has been limited.

Directives, on the other hand, are never directly applicable, they never become law automatically. On the contrary, the very purpose of a directive is to give a Member State the opportunity to fulfil the task which the EU gives it in the manner most suited to it. For instance, a directive may contain a provision requiring the protection of wild birds. A Member State may write its law in such a way as to include other wild animals as well. Member States might be unwilling to implement legislation they disagree with or they might implement it but do it incorrectly. In such cases, the Commission may take the infringing Member State to the European Court of Justice. Individuals who have suffered damage as a result of non-implementation or incorrect implementation may take their own Member State to their national courts and seek compensation.

Other forms of laws include decisions, which are only binding on those they address, and recommendations and opinions. An important source of EU law is judgments of the European Court of Justice. Although the judgments only bind the parties they address, in reality national courts follow them as precedents.

What are the basic principles of the EU?

We have seen that the Union acts in a very large number of issues and that it has considerable potential to limit national sovereignty. This ability, conferred to the EU under specific conditions, defines one of the most important features of its law – *supremacy*. The concept of supremacy, although never properly defined in the Treaty, means that EU law hierarchically comes before national law. By signing the Treaty, Member States have transferred parts of their sovereignty in certain areas onto the Union.

Supremacy manifests itself in many ways – from regulations, which become directly applicable laws in Member States, to constitutions of some Member States that have expressly provided for the EU's supremacy. In the UK, in what appears to be a modification of the doctrine of parliamentary sovereignty, the European Communities Act 1972 has expressly acknowledged that EU laws come before domestic laws. This, naturally, does not mean that a Member State can never leave the EU, but it does mean that, while it is a Member, its sovereignty has, for mutual benefit, some limitations.

The legal basis game

In order to address the problem of EU and national sovereignty, Member States have devised mechanisms to control law-making activities that happen at EU level. The main idea that embodies this principle is that the EU and its institutions only possess those powers that have been given to them. No law can be passed at EU level unless a legal basis can be found in its primary constitutional document, namely the EC Treaty. This important principle, also known as the conferral of powers, is embodied in Art 5(1), which provides that 'the Community shall act within the limits of the powers conferred upon it by this Treaty and of the objectives assigned to it therein'.

The EU law-maker's choice of the legal basis will be influenced by the law-making procedure that it faces. The law-making process in the EU is complicated but it is sufficient to say that some important constitutional decisions in the EU must be made unanimously. In other words, all Member States, voting in the Council of Ministers, must approve the measure. A majority of the decisions, however, are made by qualified majority. This means that a measure will be passed if the majority are in favour of it.

Fierce battles have been and still are fought between Member States on one side and Union institutions on the other, over the appropriate legal basis. But why is this choice so important? The paramount question is whether the EU has the capacity to act in certain cases or not. States have often claimed that the EU cannot make laws in particular areas. Competences between the Union and Member States may be described as falling into three separate categories: exclusive EU competence, competence shared between the EU and Member States, and exclusive Member States' competence. Since the EU has the capacity to act in a number of areas, the majority of law-making falls within shared competences.

Once it has been decided that the EU has the capacity to act, the question is whether a particular proposal comes within a particular competence or not. This is where the legal basis game comes in. If the EU uses a legal basis requiring only a majority vote, it will be more likely to succeed; if the legal basis requires a unanimous decision, it will be less likely to succeed. The EU will, naturally, claim that the proposal falls within a legal basis that is easier to satisfy, such as the Single Market one. Member States, eager to preserve their sovereignty, will, on the other hand, often claim that the legal basis should have been the one requiring unanimity. This would give the power to veto a proposal and entrust the Member States with greater control over EU activities. Naturally, bases requiring unanimity lead to rather poorly drafted laws, as the Commission waters down the proposal until each of the 25 States is prepared to agree to it. The importance of qualified majority voting, therefore, must be emphasised.

Subsidiarity

The relations between Member States and the EU are also reflected through another important principle – that of *subsidiarity*. This principle, the importance of which cannot be emphasised enough, is embodied in Art 5(2):

> In areas which do not fall within its exclusive competence, the Community shall take action, in accordance with the principle of subsidiarity, only if and in so far as the objectives of the proposed action cannot be sufficiently achieved by the Member States and can therefore, by reason of the scale or effects of the proposed action, be better achieved by the Community.

Looking at this provision we first notice that it only operates in areas where the EU does not have exclusive competence. Being a principle that strikes a balance between Union and national areas of capacity, subsidiarity does not operate where this balance has, by default, been shifted completely in favour of the EU. This, however, is only true in very few areas, such as common commercial policy or fisheries.

The EU, even when it does have a legal basis, can only act if the proposed action cannot be achieved at the Member State level. This must be understood to mean also regional, and even local level. For example, issues such as waste collection or recycling, even when they fall under one of the bases in the Treaty, can often better be dealt with at a local level. What determines whether action can be sufficiently achieved is its scale or effect. The most obvious, but not the only, manifestation of subsidiarity is the obligation to use a directive, rather than a regulation, since the former enables Member States to achieve the proposed aim though their own means. In addition to this, Art 5(3) provides that 'Any action by the Community shall not go beyond what is necessary to achieve the objectives of this Treaty'. This is referred to as the principle of proportionality. EU action should only go as far as is necessary to achieve the goal that it seeks.

The EU was set up as an economic organisation. In the course of its history, it has become necessary to grant protection of fundamental rights. Part of the reason for this was the concern of some Member States that a union of such scope and depth cannot allow itself to exist without legal protection of some commonly accepted values. It is important to understand, however, that fundamental rights were never the main purpose of the EC Treaty. A cursory look would be enough to establish the fact that even a basic list of these is missing. Recently, documents such as the Charter of Fundamental Rights have been drafted specifically to address these shortcomings of the Treaty. More importantly, however, the European Court of Justice has recognised early the necessity to address the rights – in an early set of cases, it has said that those derive from constitutional orders of Member States. Finally, it is worth saying that the parallel systems of protection of fundamental rights, such as the European Convention on Human Rights, are perceived as complementary and not opposed.

Direct effect

The principles that EU law rely on are numerous. Some have a firm basis in the Treaty, others are general principles derived from national law (such as effectiveness or access to justice). Other yet are developed thorough the European Court of Justice's creative interpretation of the sources of EU law. Among these, few have more importance for the effectiveness of EU law than the concept of *direct effect*. Direct effect is the capacity of an individual to rely on EU law in their national courts. Applicants who can avail themselves of EU law as if it was their own national law are clearly in a better position than if these rights are only accessible to them through unfamiliar EU institutions. It was, in fact, so important for the EU to be able to protect its law effectively that the European Court of Justice thought it necessary to introduce this feature where a real basis in the Treaty did not exist. In the now famous C-26/62 *Van Gend en Loos* case, which happened early in the development of EU law, the Court of Justice said that the EU would not be functional if individuals were not in the position to rely on rights granted to them.

Not all provisions of EU law have direct effect. In order to be directly effective, a provision must be sufficiently clear and precise and confer rights on individuals. Conditional provisions, or those that grant discretion to administrative authorities, for instance, will not have that capacity. It follows that not even all Treaty provisions have direct effect. Those that do not are enforceable at EU level through EU remedies, but not in national courts. The biggest problem was presented by directives. These, as was pointed out earlier, have to be implemented into national law, and Member States enjoy considerable flexibility as to the means of such implementation. It is clear that directives have direct effect, once they have been implemented. This effect is given to them through national law.

But, what will happen if the directive is not implemented, or is implemented improperly, and the deadline has passed? For example, a (fictitious) EU directive gives all students the right to government-funded free laptops for the duration of their course. A Member State implements the directive, but in such a way that excludes the students on part-time courses. A disgruntled student could not avail herself of the directive, as it has not been properly implemented. She can petition the EU institutions to follow one of the paths open to them in the Treaty, but from her own perspective, this solution is neither elegant nor particularly fast. What the concept of direct effect provides her with is the possibility to rely on the provisions of the directive as if they were properly implemented. This will take place in an action against the Member State, in the courts of the Member State, once the deadline for implementation has passed. The State will therefore not be able to benefit from its own improper action.

What does the EU regulate?

The European Union regulates widely, on a number of issues within its competence. Indeed, this has often been one of the main criticisms levelled against it – that it does too much and it goes too deep. But to be able to understand if this is really the case, we need to look into one of the most important areas in the EU, namely the law of the Single Market.

Single Market

As has been indicated earlier, although it is not easy to summarise the activities of the European Union accurately, one can define it as the free flow of economic factors, in pursuit of greater prosperity of the State and its citizens. To reach this goal, it was necessary to enable the free movement of goods, services, people and capital, and the law of the Single Market plays a key role there by removing the barriers that Member States might otherwise impose.

Article 12 prohibits discrimination on the basis of nationality and is one of the fundamental provisions of the EC Treaty. However, on its own it would not suffice to ensure free movement of factors of production for the simple reason that not all barriers discriminate. For instance, a prohibition on discrimination would make illegal any measure in State A imposing a total ban or a quota on toys from State B. But that provision would not prevent a measure that mandates that all toys sold in State B be packaged in recyclable material, even if such measure can in practice act as a ban or at least make the export of toys to State B more expensive. This difficulty has largely been eliminated in EU law through the concept known as 'home country control'. According to this, a product or a service is allowed to access markets of other Member States if it has lawfully been made or provided in the State of origin (Home State). Host State rules that present a barrier to this movement will be illegal unless justified by a set of specifically provided rules in the EC Treaty.

Free movement of goods

The European Union is a customs union. This means that Member States have removed customs barriers between themselves and introduced a common customs policy towards other countries. Customs duties are, therefore, prohibited between Member States. On the other hand, as Art 90 of the EC Treaty provides, the States are free to tax as long as they do not discriminate towards other Member States. Therefore, Member State A will be able to tax cars at a rate that is twice as high as in Member State B, provided that it taxes all cars equally – imported as well as those produced domestically.

In addition to prohibiting customs duties and discriminatory taxes, the EC Treaty, in Art 28, prohibits quotas and 'measures having equivalent effect'. But what are measures having equivalent effect and how do they affect trade between Member States? The Treaty does not answer these questions and the European Court of Justice has over several decades provided detailed case law interpreting Art 28. In a well-known series of cases beginning with C-8/74 *Dassonville*, continuing with C-120/78 *Cassis de Dijon* and culminating in C-267/91 *Keck and Mithouard*, the European Court of Justice has said that discriminatory and non-discriminatory rules of Member States (therefore not actions of private corporations or individuals) that hinder trade shall be illegal.

Discriminatory rules distinguish between national and imported goods in law and in fact. A prohibition of imports imposed by State A on goods from State B is directly discriminatory but restrictions do not have to take the shape of prohibitions or quotas. A Member State can lead advertising and promoting campaigns that favour domestic products, or it can impose higher prices or more stringent conditions (such as health inspections) on imported goods. The key to discrimination is that domestic products are not subject to the added difficulties, and are therefore put at an advantage.

Non-discriminatory rules that hinder trade do not distinguish in law but do so in fact. They impose a higher burden on the importer due to the additional work it has to complete to make the product marketable. Although in law the rules apply equally to domestic producers and importers, in reality the burden is born by importers, the domestic producers already complying with the rules. If, in addition, the product is marketed in a number of Member States, the exporter from State B might be subject to as many different regimes as there are countries into which he is hoping to import.

For example, a (fictitious) law in State A states that alcoholic drinks of a particular kind must not contain more than 20% alcohol. The producer from State B makes and regularly exports drinks of this kind which contain 25% alcohol. It will be observed that the law in State A applies to all those who wish to market the alcoholic drinks in question – whether they are domestic in origin or foreign. In that respect, *in law*, State A does not discriminate. On the other hand, as a result of the presence of that law, a legally marketed drink from State B either has to be modified and its alcohol contents reduced to only 20% or it must be absent from the market of State A altogether. EU law, under the circumstances mentioned in the previous paragraph, prohibits this kind of distinction: however, although *the law* appears to treat all parties equally, *in fact* domestic producers are favoured.

Naturally, allegations can be made against any rule that inconveniences the trader, and this includes a very large number of rules. Therefore, in the last of the mentioned cases, *Keck*, and those that followed it, the European Court of Justice decided that only rules relating to product requirements (shape, size, colour, etc) should be illegal, while those relating to selling arrangements (opening hours, staff training requirements, etc) will mostly not be. The division was an attempt to limit the number of cases to only those situations where, in the absence of discrimination, there is real danger of the importer being subjected simultaneously to rules of several States.

Under certain circumstances, Member States whose rules have been disapplied may defend them. For rules that discriminate, a defence will be possible under Art 30 which mentions, among other things, public health or public morality. For example, a restriction of import of meat from certain countries will be legal if it has clear medical grounds. A restriction of importation of pornographic material may be justified if such material is normally not available in the said Member State. Non-discriminatory rules may be justified not only by reference to Art 30 but also to a list of exceptions made by the European Court of Justice. This list of 'mandatory requirements' is wider than Art 30, as it is meant to give Host States more space to defend their own rules.

Free movement of persons

Broadly defined, this freedom enables citizens of one Member State to travel to others, alone or with their families, to work there (permanently or temporarily), to visit places as tourists or simply to live. The idea behind EU legislation in this field is that citizens from other Member States should be treated *equally* with domestic ones – they should not be discriminated against. In this era of cheap travel and raised cultural awareness it is perhaps easy to forget the true impact of this provision that creates a big borderless space, open to workers as well as to students and tourists.

The operation of the Treaty provisions on freedom of movement of workers is best explained by a few examples.

> Helen, a qualified biologist, is a British national who wants to work in Belgium. She specialises in yeast production and wants to work in a brewery. On 1 April 2005, she travels to Brussels with her American husband, Ross, and their two children. On arrival she is told by the authorities that, as she does not have a Belgian diploma, she can only work as a lab technician and not a consultant, as she had

hoped. This means a much smaller salary. Unhappy with that arrangement, Helen starts working part-time as a climbing instructor but is often out of work. After six months, the Belgian authorities send her a letter saying that 'due to persistent unemployment' she is required to leave Belgium immediately.

Ross, in the meantime, applies for work as a translator in the Ministry of Defence. He is rejected on the ground that jobs in the Ministry are vital to national security and are open only to Belgian nationals and also because Ross only speaks French whereas the posts are open only to those who speak both French and Flemish.

Upon arrival, Helen and Ross apply for child maintenance support, to enable them to put their children in day care. They are rejected, as both of them are unemployed.

Let us examine Helen and Ross's situation and any rights they may have under EU law. It may be worth noting that both of them have rights and obligations that derive from Belgian law (in the same manner that someone from Japan may have a valid work and residence permit in Belgium). Before EU law 'intervened', Helen and Ross would have to rely on Belgian law to regulate their status. This law, like that of any other Member State, would not necessarily be difficult to satisfy, but would not grant equal treatment with Belgian nationals. In this lies the great contribution of EU law to free movement of persons. Ideally, they, as a British couple from, say, Cambridge, would be treated equally before Belgian authorities as a Belgian couple from Charleroi.

Building on the general prohibition of discrimination in Art 12, Art 39 provides:

Article 39

1. Freedom of movement for workers shall be secured within the Community.

2. Such freedom of movement shall entail the abolition of any discrimination based on nationality between workers of the Member States as regards employment, remuneration and other conditions of work and employment.

3. It shall entail the right, subject to limitations justified on grounds of public policy, public security or public health:

(a) to accept offers of employment actually made;

(b) to move freely within the territory of Member States for this purpose;

(c) to stay in a Member State for the purpose of employment in accordance with the provisions governing the employment of nationals of that State laid down by law, regulation or administrative action;

(d) to remain in the territory of a Member State after having been employed in that State, subject to conditions which shall be embodied in implementing regulations to be drawn up by the Commission.

Helen and Ross's first problem is looming deportation. A good lawyer would almost certainly try to keep the couple in the country while their case is argued on substance. This has always been possible under EU law and in this case the lawyer would ask for a provisional measure to keep them in Belgium while they contest the deportation order. But what is their status? What will they actually say once they come before a Belgian court?

Let us first look at Helen's rights under the Treaty and any secondary legislation. First, Helen has a right to look for work. She does not need to have a job offer and neither is she required to obtain a work permit or a residence permit prior to coming to Belgium and starting her job. She is therefore entitled to move to Belgium without having a specific job in mind, simply with finding work in mind.

How long is Helen entitled to stay in Belgium if she were only a work seeker? From a handful of cases at the European Court of Justice, we know that a Member State is entitled to impose a time limit, such as six months in Belgium. A work seeker, however, would be entitled to stay in the country even after this deadline, provided that he or she keeps looking for work and has a genuine chance of being engaged. This is clearly Helen's case, as she continues working as an instructor, even with frequent breaks. But, from the facts, we know that she is not only a work seeker but also a worker. There are two issues we have to deal with: first, the limitation of her employment possibilities, and, secondly, 'persistent unemployment' as the basis of deportation.

Articles 12 and 39 of the EC Treaty and subsequent legislation and case law of the European Court of Justice provide that foreign workers must not be discriminated against. Discrimination may take a direct form, as in 'only Italian nationals may work on Italian railways' or a more subtle, indirect form, such as in our example. Helen is refused work, not because she is not Belgian, but because she does not have a Belgian diploma. Although it is not impossible for her to obtain one, the burden of additional education and training is unreasonable and may even prove impossible. Therefore, she, as a British national, is put at a disadvantage compared with Belgian nationals. In other words, her position would have been different, but for the fact that she is foreign. The discrimination is indirect but present and effective. Helen would, therefore, be able to challenge Belgian legislation successfully.

The second issue is her status after she was told that she could not work as a consultant. She finds part-time work as a climbing instructor. Does this work bring her under the protection of the Treaty? The European Court of Justice's answer to this has continually been positive. Any work qualifies, as long as workers are properly compensated. Therefore, part-time work (consisting even of just a few hours per week) qualifies. Helen's status is, therefore, that of a worker. Even if we take into account the fact that she is 'often out of work', at worst, her status fluctuates between that of a worker and that of a work seeker.

What rights does Ross have? He is not an EU national but an American. If we followed common logic, we would conclude that Ross does not have any EU rights whatsoever, but that he may have some rights under Belgian law. This is only partially true. As a matter of fact, Ross, as a *family member* of an EU citizen (Helen), has a number of rights that are not direct, but derive from Helen's rights. The logic behind this is that, if the economic and political goal is to enable easy migration from one EU country to another, that migration is more likely to take place if EU nationals are allowed to take their family members with them under the same conditions that apply to them. Ross would, therefore, be able to avail himself of the same benefits that apply to Helen. He would be able to enter Belgium freely, look for work and take up employment on a par with Belgian citizens.

But here, his job application at the Ministry of Defence is rejected on the grounds of national security and of language requirements. Although the first ground seems to be discriminatory, Art 39(4) of the EC Treaty provides that 'the provisions of this article shall not apply to employment in the public service'. The European Court of Justice has interpreted 'public service' to include positions of national security, but has also included the civil service (such as HM Revenue & Customs) and other similar positions in it. Depending on the nature of the job Ross is applying for, the authorities' rejection would probably be justified.

But, can they require him to speak both French and Flemish? The European Court of Justice has decided in the past that Member States may impose reasonable language requirements. A person may be required to speak a language up to a certain standard, if that language is necessary in the course of work. A doctor may, therefore, be required to speak both English and Gaelic in Ireland, if there is a significant proportion of patients speaking Gaelic. In Ross's case, the Belgian requirement to speak two languages may be deemed to be non-discriminatory and reasonable, in light of the fact that Belgium is bilingual and that Government administration in particular functions in both languages.

Helen and Ross have applied for child maintenance support. The question is, what is the range of rights to which nationals of Member States are entitled when working abroad? The EC Treaty did not regulate this, but important subsequent EU laws have. Regulation 1612/68 provides that other EU 'workers' shall enjoy the same 'social and tax advantages' as nationals. The European Court of Justice has extended the scope of this provision to include family members and it has even applied it to other freedoms (establishment and services). In order to qualify for child maintenance support, Helen and Ross would have to be 'economically active' – they would have to be workers or work seekers. In their present situation, Helen, at least, should be treated as a worker, in spite of the temporary nature of such work. She would then be able to claim not only child support, but also the Belgian equivalent of tax credit, jobseeker's allowance and a range of other benefits normally open to nationals.

But, the obvious question is, what happens if Helen stops working at some point? Does she automatically lose all her rights under the EC Treaty? Should she not then be entitled, at least, to jobseeker's allowance? Until recently, the situation was unclear. However, in one of the more recent revisions of the Treaty, provisions on EU citizenship were added (EC Treaty, Arts 17–22). On their own, they were little more than a political declaration, devoid of real power. However, this is not how the European Court of Justice interpreted them. In a few important rulings, it said that nationals of Member States who are lawfully residing in the territory of another Member State have the right to rely on Art 12 (prohibition on discrimination based on nationality) simply on account of the fact that they are *EU citizens*. They do not have to be economically active. Therefore, in our example, if Helen lost her job, she would still be entitled to all social and tax benefits.

Naturally, Member States are very concerned that this development might encourage a lot of benefit claimers who have no real economic connection with the State to claim. At present, however, it is clear that the European Court of Justice is not prepared to allow this. It interprets the provisions of the Treaty in a more restrictive manner, not enabling them to take on the power that they would normally have in a federation (such as the United States or Canada).

Council Directive 2004/38 further clarifies the rights of EU citizens and their family members to move to and reside in other Member States. This provision does not replace EC

Treaty Articles and case law on workers or citizens but clarifies it. It enables any EU citizen to reside freely in another Member State, up to three months, without any formalities except presenting a valid ID upon entering the country. Stays of longer than three months are allowed for workers, those who have sufficient means to support themselves, students and dependent family members.

Conclusion

In summary, the European Union has taken upon itself many tasks. It can no longer be described simply as an economic organisation. Its basis remains the decision of Member States to transfer parts of their sovereignty to a larger community. This transfer, at the same time, remains the most contentious issue in the EU, with the border between competences being freshly questioned. At the same time, the tension between widening (more Member States) versus deepening (more competences) of the Union has become very important. But, irrespective of the future of this particular embodiment of Europe, its half-a-century-old legacy of cooperation seems to have left a lasting impact.

Reading list

D Chalmers et al, *European Union Law: Text and Materials* (Cambridge University Press, 2006).

P Craig & C de Búrca, *EU Law: Text, Cases and Materials* (3rd edn, Oxford: Oxford University Press, 2003).

T Hartley, *Foundations of European Community Law* (5th edn, Oxford: Oxford University Press, 2003).

Index